Black Lives Matter

Black Lives Matter
Poems for a New World

Edited by Ambrose Musiyiwa

Civic  Leicester

First published in Great Britain in 2020 by
CivicLeicester

CivicLeicester

y. https://www.youtube.com/user/CivicLeicester

f. https://www.facebook.com/CivicLeicester

CivicLeicester@gmail.com

ISBN-13: 978-1-9164593-5-9

Dedicated to all who insist that Black Lives Matter

Contents

Introduction

IN MAY 2020, George Floyd's murder was captured on a mobile phone video by active bystanders. The video showed a white policeman pressing his knee against Floyd's neck and keeping it there for close to nine minutes until Floyd died. The murder triggered months of mass protests in the United States and around the world.

The protests have been taking place in the midst of a global pandemic that, in Europe and the United States, is also disproportionately killing people from Black, Asian and ethnic minority backgrounds.

An entry on Wikipedia highlights how "Black Lives Matter", "Hands up, don't shoot", "Am I a threat?", "I can't breathe", "White silence is violence", "No justice, no peace", "Is my son next?", "Get your knee off my neck", and more, have become rallying calls against the killing of Black people by the police and against racism, racialised inequality, discrimination, violence and oppression.

Around the world people are demanding justice and change.

Black Lives Matter: Poems for a New World came out of a call, which was issued in June 2020, for poems and short prose on the theme, "Black Lives Matter."

We were looking for submissions exploring any of the images, issues, triggers, histories, lives, demands and outcomes that are being highlighted by Black Lives Matter and current and past protests. And we were interested in submissions from writers of all ages and backgrounds, based anywhere in the world.

We received close to 500 poems from over 300 writers around the world. The anthology, *Black Lives Matter* presents 107 of these poems. The poems were selected for how they respond to the theme and how they speak to others in the anthology.

I commend these poems to you and hope they will also encourage you to look at your village, town, region and country as well as your school, college, university, club, association or workplace and the places you get goods and services from and insist that Black Lives Matter in these spaces as well.

Ambrose Musiyiwa
Leicester, November 2020

Species of Reply/Einstein Wasn't Wrong

To witness the wordspill I could hardly wait.
Would he accept that Denial's Not Appropriate?
And for a moment he acknowledges the reality
seeming to experience nanoseconds of clarity
confirming a partial apparent acceptance
of solid scientific evidence that the
first modern Briton was black, black.
But then makes sure his interpretation
of the incontrovertible revelation pleases
those affected by jingoistic diseases

(finding these words)

I belong here, this is twenty eighteen
Nothing to fear from a Mesolithic fossil
(Nothing against him but nothing in common)
Struggling a bit with the DNA findings though,
Cheddar Man sounds more light than dark to me
However, for the sake of discussion let's say
this minor blip occurred way back, back
in a time so distant
that it's almost irrelevant
Luckily during ten thousand years
of British history this glitch was erased
from our proud ancestry
but if it had not

(he concludes)

It is recorded that, in 1946, Albert Einstein stood in front of students at Lincoln University, the oldest historically black college in the United States, and during a commencement speech declared, "There is separation of coloured people from white people in the United States. That separation is not a disease of coloured people. It is a disease of white people. I do not intend to be quiet about it."

Cheddar Man, Britain's oldest complete human skeleton, was excavated in 1903 at Gough's Cave in the Cheddar Gorge, Somerset, England. The remains date from the Mesolithic period (circa 7100 BC). DNA analysis indicates that he was a typical member of the Western European population of the time. Although he had light coloured eyes his hair was dark brown or black and his skin was dark or black.

a nightmarish tragedy
which doesn't bear thinking about
Imagine me and my people, still proudly
patriotic but dark of colour, having to yell at
paler people (nothing against them but nothing
in common) that they should go back, back
to where they came from, to where they
belong, not upon this sceptred isle,
this green and pleasant land

Peter A

Martyr for Humanity

She went live on Facebook saying that she was sorry for the family of the deceased but his face was not worthy to be painted on walls. He was a druggie she said not a martyr. Quoting an academic, in ivy-league tones, she argued that the Black race is the only race that celebrates dysfunction.

"You are an example to your community," a southern belle wrote in the chat, inspired by this young African-American woman.

"Your Community?" I thought, logging off.

Hopefully she, from my community, will one day understand how it is that George Floyd is a Martyr for Humanity.

'Funmi Adewole

Black Skin

What do they see
When they look at black skin?
Do they see gang members?
Drug dealers?
A thug with a knife?
Do they see unruly hair?
An unruly child?
A trouble maker?
A thief?
A criminal?
A convict?
A threat?
Do they see a story on the news of a person we've never met?
Do they see the worst of us
In all of us?
The second they see black skin
What if they paused?
Gave a second look?
What could they see?
They could see our pain
They could see our struggle
They could see how far we've risen
They could see the lives we have
The futures we could have
Not just the ones they put on us
They could see doctors and lawyers
Writers and artists
Scientists and leaders
They could see all the things we truly are
And all the things we could become
They could see us the way they see themselves
They could see hopes
They could see dreams
A life that matters
And then maybe they would no longer choose to end that life
Just because they see black skin

Mayo Agard-Olubo

4

Am I A Threat? Part One

Am I A Threat?
Why?
When
I birthed the World within my treasured lands.
I created Axum, Ethiopia,
where the Ark of the Covenant now sleeps.
I stood with the Black Nubians of Kush.
I built the Pyramids of Ancient Egypt.
I crossed the desert highways of Ghana, Mali and Songhai
with bountiful riches and tales of wonder and gods.
I marched with Roman armies as commander and soldier,
building roads, walls and cities like Londinium; yes, London.
I forged the Benin Bronzes and carved drums to beat
the hearts of my people, then and now.
I moulded the Ashanti Stool of a nation. Our Sunsum: our spirit; our soul.
I shaped Great Zimbabwe out of earth and stone.
I rallied with Robert Wedderburn against the horrors
endured by the enslaved on the streets of England.
I survived countless treacherous crossings in choppy oceans, shackles,
chains, sweat and blood.
I became the Black Jacobins,
leading a revolution in Saint Domingue
now known as Haiti.
I knew Nanny and Tacky of the Maroons, Paul Bogle, Sam Sharpe,
Cuffy of Guyana, Zumbi of Brazil;
all who paved the way to freedom in the sun.
I wore the crown as Nefertiti, Cleopatra, Queen Nzinga, Yaa Asantewa,
Mary Seacole, Sojourner Truth, Harriet Tubman,
Phillis Wheatley, Claudia Jones…

I spoke of John Henry, Henry Box Brown, Marcus Garvey, Malcolm X,
Martin Luther King, Patrice Lumumba, Walter Rodney…

I bare witness to the lives of Emmett Till, Ahmaud Arbery, George Floyd,
Breonna Taylor, Atatiana Jefferson, Stephon Clark, Eric Garner, Sandra Bland,
Tamir Rice, Michael Brown, Rodney King, Mark Duggan, Sean Rigg,
Jean Charles de Menezes, Rashan Charles, Joy Gardner, Cynthia Jarrett,
Cherry Groce, The New Cross Thirteen, Stephen Lawrence…
And all those whose names are lost in Time and hang lifeless on
twisted trees.

An endless... endless list that haunts and torments
a World where Justice is muted... silent... unjust... empty.

Really... and you see me as The Threat?
Am I A Threat?
Am I?
Am I?
Am I?

(Fade Out)

Sandra A Agard

Other Viruses and Diseases

As Spring came it brought with it
a deadly contagion
that spread across many lands
as the first buds burst through.

And this coronavirus exposed other
equally virulent viruses, revealing
the deep-seated sicknesses
that have affronted many nations.

The virus of racism is transmitted
through orchestrated fear and ignorance,
fomented by the demented voices
that require division to stay in power.

In the past it was cramped ships
with chains, enforced labour, white hoods
and frightening crosses of fire, segregation;
now it is cramped jails, the knee on the neck.

But this virus like the *Yersinia Pestis* bacterium
that carried the plague from infected fleas on rats
or *Plasmodium falciparum* that infects mosquitoes
that infect us with malaria both reveal their sources.

For the fear of the foreign or other through race,
through religion or division by age or by class,
or by gender keeps everyone at everyone else's
throats while they keep their hands firmly on the till.

And what we really need is a vaccine for Capital;
for the greed that consumes the entire planet
so that none of us can breathe. If applied well
fresh air will surely flow with justice and with peace.

Jim Aitken

Breathless

in this time   when even
breathing is a danger
breathless

from running hard just to be
at the back of the pack
breathless

from the hundreds of years
bearing down on your chest
breathless

breathe   less
take up less space do not be
so obvious   so demanding

breathe   less
stand quietly in the shadows
do not ask for your share

breathe   less
try not to draw attention to yourself
as you go about your business

but if you are waiting
for things to change

do not hold your breath
instead   draw it all in

and blow this house down

Nick Allen

Colston's toppled statue at daybreak, June 11th 2020

Today the M Shed bears a strange fruit
wrapped in blue tarpaulin, tied with pale blue string
a lime green tractor has hauled the strange fruit in.

Rosalie Alston

Oware

She wipes chocolate crumbs off her mouth. I know about fatty shame. She sets the board, dark and slightly lumpy, between us. In each house sit four beans. "White kidney," she says without looking up. Her phone's on. Her hand, beans and mental arithmetic flash past me. She captures my e, d, and c. I don't want to disappoint her so I struggle on. "Is it legal to use a calculator?" "No," she says, staring down at the board. I see the corners of her lips rise towards her cheeks and imagine the devil in her eyes.

Judith Amanthis

Jummah prayer under the olive tree

I was 18 when I made it to Libya. On the first Friday, I left the camp and walked far to the mosque. I arrived early and sat in the front row. People gathered, and when we stood up for Sallah prayer, someone pulled me back. "You don't belong here, go to the back." On the next Friday, I walked to the sea, and I prayed under an olive tree. I asked God, "Are we, black people, of less value?" I heard the rustling of the olive tree I would have to leave behind and the sea waves I would have to cross.

A man who wishes to remain anonymous and Alexandros Plasatis

Say Their Names

Say their names, keep them alive
We must remember, not ignore
Those who have fallen victim
To a brand-new civil war.

George Floyd, Breonna Taylor
Ahmaud Arbery are only just a few
Of the many lives that were taken
In hate, unjust, needless and undue.

Say their names, never forget
Let's all help to break the chain
Of violence, bigotry, and hatred
So they will not have died in vain.

Adrienne Asher

They Matter

I heard the old lynching laws
were never repealed.
That they still stand
like strong southern trees -
and who swings from these
as if it didn't matter?

In such statutes fates of lives are sealed.
Here is the strange fruit of an old disease.
Black men and boys
still being deleted.
and history is repeated
and history is repeated.

A hole in the chest
a shot to the head.
A mother distressed
as her child watches
a white vest turn red
watches a man alive
become dead
as if it doesn't matter.

A shot in the back
as a boy runs away
under attack
for staying out too long
in the wrong place
for wearing the wrong face.

His attacker gets off on a replay
His attacker gets off on a replay
as if it didn't matter.

As headlines become bylines
bystanders grow tired
So Black lives get sidelined
as if they never mattered.

Turning into stories

to be kicked around
to service politicians' aims
media games
picking out pieces to inflame
as if they were on a mission
to make things stay the same.

Meanwhile in real time
Black men break laws unwritten.
Forgetting, they do the things forbidden.
Like reaching in pockets for mobile phones.
Like walking out late.
Like walking alone.
Like remembering that they're free
but forgetting that freedom shouldn't be exhibited too freely.

What freedom is that? Freedom in tatters
When land of the free can't see Black life matters.

From the Supreme Court to the roadside cop
we see those that ought to protect
perpetuate violence.
What justice is this when guns don't stop?
When your skin gets you redefined as a threat
there's no time for silence.
No time to pretend it doesn't matter.
In time what matters to one matters to all.
We see them fall.
They matter.

Mellow Baku

Black Queens

In my reflection I see the strong black women who built their legacy.
Black queens who worked tirelessly and silently with cloaks of invisibility.
In their image I stand unapologetically.
No longer silent, no longer invisible.
No longer exhausted from playing small or being made to feel disposable.
Today I break the cycle for future generations.
Smart, creative, fearlessly owning my black excellence.
I am her, she is me. Authentically we speak in unity. We are and always
will be, black queens.

Sharon Cherry Ballard

I am so grateful

I am so grateful to be in this space
I am so grateful for the opportunities it could create
that I allow the space to dictate and stagnate whilst the frustration collates.

I am so grateful that I bow my head in silence
I am so grateful I tame down my vibrance
like a voodoo witch stealing away the voice of a siren
I allow it to act as a tyrant and enable it to become my asylum.

I am so grateful that I am no longer sure what it is I'm grateful for
as I evolve past my conditioning it's clear to see that without my presence
the space is simply a few walls and a door
and the more I explore, my sanity begins to restore and I REALISE that I
am truly grateful once more.

Sharon Cherry Ballard

Little girl
Inspired by the life of Maya Angelou

Do not feel scared little girl
Tell your stories proudly, they need to be heard and only you can find those
authentic words.
Do not hide away little girl
Your words are more powerful than they will have your care, it will touch
millions of hearts and answer many prayers.
Do not doubt yourself little girl
You're part of a larger picture, you're more than a verse or even a
scripture.
Speak loudly little girl
So all can hear, you were put on this earth to speak without fear and
through many tears you'll persevere to inspire the lives of those you hold
dear.

Sharon Cherry Ballard

Streets Paved with Gold

She lived in the same flat
for forty years
until she cracked
spilling to the four walls

of a splintered house
that echoed.
She wanted to spit
back in their faces.

Sometime in the future
she may be remembered
for more than a moment,
as more than just a stack

of untold narratives
boxed and shelved.
She spent her time worn to a glob.
Trying to make the dream work

filling family back home
with Mother Country's promise
of building sprawling manors.
After that, she used her days

learning how to swallow tears
until they streamed inside her
pushed against her innards.
She couldn't find a valve.

I heard she once girted her neck so tight,
to keep it all from spilling out,
that she split her gut.
She has never been the same.

Panya Banjoko

This black body

This is how
They wage war on the black body
They get you from the outside in
Until it becomes inside out

They tell you   you are not wanted
They teach you to hate this black body
The deep brown eyes
The black curls between the thighs
The wide set nose
And thick lips that curve into a frown
The curly hair that should only be seen as a crown
Strong arms and strong legs add fuel to the fire

Tanisha Barrett

Forgetting blackness

Do I pass?
Can I make you forget my blackness
Through education
Or art?
Maybe money will do it?
Or the postcode of my address
That jumble of numbers and letters
Might make you forget?
Protect me from your violence, your malice
Maybe if I talk like you
Straighten my hair so the coils fall in line
Will you see less of it then?
Will that make my blackness disappear?
Can I pass?
Will you let me pass?

Tanisha Barrett

Photo-op from the White House to St John's

What monuments for Ahmaud, Breonna and George
and all who have died in 'the land of the free'
at the hands of vigilantes or the police?

Police, who fired rubber bullets and teargas
for a president who thrives on the smoke

blown-up his ass by White House sycophants
as he panders to his base
instincts, in allegiance with the religious cult
of 'white America'
convinced that a stunt with a bible
will bring him closer to a second coming.

The 'book' converted to his accessory
for stoking racism, which has held bloated white limbs
on the throat of black people - unable to breathe freely

since Spain then Britain 'discovered' America.

Reversing its mirror to the savagery
pulsing beneath white skins,
they racially replaced Indigenous Indians.

Then returned to Africa to clap the limbs
and hearts and minds of black people in irons
in their millions, reducing them
to entries in British plantation owners' ledgers.

Now the streets we tread to protest racism
bear these names and statues of world-leading slavers
and colonists, who sired America's grotesque birth defect

which has found its greatest expression in a president
who can barely string an uncorrupted sentence together
other than to defend his own thin Scottish/German skin.

In a paler reflection of him, the British Prime Minister
attempts similar cultural wars

while those piss-poor flabby white men
who voted for him, will never hear him reflect
on 'Operation Legacy's' effect on our 'real' history.

Nor will they uncover enough facts
for their conspiracy theories to fill the back of a Deep South
fag packet, while pissing on monuments they claim to defend.

They contend the problems lie with black people,
perhaps for fear they might march on white supremacists
and become murdering sons of bitches
just like them.

Lesley Benzie

Invisible Ballad

I, too, with Langston sing Scotland
And pray for liberty with Emily.
One flesh was made to cover all the land.

I dream of the fearsome frigates we manned
And burn them out of God's eye.
I, too, with Langston sing Scotland

When they greeted with a whip, I would with a hand
And face my Ulysses with no lies:
One flesh was made to cover all the land.

I hate wearing anything monochrome -
Every colour here makes me feel at home.

Even your 'Christ' would understand
No matter what verses you claim he says.
I, too, with Langston sing Scotland.

I know his truth better than any man
The truth that washes over all mankind:
One flesh was made to cover all the land.

I hate wearing anything monochrome -
Every colour here makes me feel at home.
I share my words with Hurston in the end
Because Larkin's ears belong in the tomb.
I, too, for Langston sing for true Scotland
And all flesh was made to cover the land.

Conor Blessing

Never Ending Battle

They think the politicians care, that they are aware
That Black Lives Matter.
But, it's plain to see, in this democracy,
The time is not right to lance the boil of royal white supremacy.
Of Eton Boys, polo, rugby, stocks and shares,
No time to declare, "Hands up, don't shoot",
Black colour is not the route to being a part
Of a system built on colonial days and fascist ways.
"Am I a threat?" to this state?
I wish I was, that Black people were,
That we could stir discontent in this nation.
"I can't breathe", I am cornered in,
Right wing politic and sin.
"White silence is violence", but in my defence,
I have no voice, no rallying call,
"No justice, no peace", and I fall.
I cannot change the diagnosis of Black,
With prognosis that lacks hope,
Just white punks and dope.
"Is my son next?",
"Get your knee off my neck",
Police brutality, fears, and tears of blood,

Tim Bombdog

Part of the Natural Order

(Bristol 1740, Leicester 2020)

When my father and mother make manacles and chains
And all the men I work with manufacture slave ship fittings
And this is the only way we know to earn a living,
Do I accept it as right, as part of the natural order?

When I know Colston's School for the poor, the Sugar House,
Merchant Venturers' Almshouses, Her Ladyship's Queen Square Mansion,
Are all founded, financed, on money from The Trade,
Do I accept it as right, as part of the natural order?

When the Minister of my Church tells me slavery
Is the only way Africans can be saved, tells me
St Paul bids slaves, "Be obedient to your masters",
Do I accept it as right, as part of the natural order?

When prelates, politicians, sugar house owners, the Mayor
All tell us the city's prosperity, stability,
Slaves' and citizens' welfare, depend upon The Trade,
Do I accept it as right, as part of the natural order?

When intellectuals, great men of the universities,
Expound their theories that Africans are only
One step above senseless beasts in the Great Chain of Being,
Do I accept it as right, as part of the natural order?

And now, in 2020, do I act on my belief that Black Lives Matter,
Bend my knee in deep respect, treasure our journey together?
What injustices, inequalities, do I still take for granted?
What, today, do I still accept without question, accept

As part of the natural order?

Richard Byrt

Acknowledgements and thanks for information from the following sources:

Lines 5 and 6. Buildings constructed in the late seventeenth and early eighteenth centuries, on the proceeds of slavery, are referred to in these lines. Sources include:

Bristol City Council Museum Collections. (Undated). St Peter's Sugar House. www.museums.bristol.gov.uk/narratives.php?im=2418

Destination Bristol. (2020). Visit Bristol. Queen Square. www.visitbristol.co.uk/things-to-do/queen-square-p38651

Historic England (2020) Merchants Adventurers' Almshouses, King Street, Bristol https://historicengland.org.uk/services-skills/education/educational-images/merchant-venturers-almshouses-king-street-5715

Turner, C. (2017). Headteacher of school founded by slave trader Edward Colston says he refuses to "obscure history" by changing its name. The Telegraph. www.telegraph.co.uk/education/2017/11/02/headteacher-school-funded-slavetrader-edward-colston

Line 11. The passage quoted, with acknowledgements and thanks, is from: Bible Gateway. (Undated). St Paul's Epistle to the Ephesians, Chapter 6, Verse 5. King James Version of the Bible: www.biblegateway.com/passage/?search=Ephesians+6%3A5%2CEphesians+6%3A6&version=KJV:~:text=...

Line 19. Some philosophers postulated the Great Chain of Being: a hierarchy ranging from God at the top to non-animate objects at the bottom. Within this hierarchy, people of different "races" and ethnicities were ranked, with black people ranked lowest and just above animals. The Great Chain of Being was used by some people to justify slavery and discriminatory beliefs and actions towards black people (Marks, J. (Updated 2020. Great Chain of Being. In: Encyclopedia.com www.encyclopedia.com/social-sciences/encyclopedias-almanacs-transcripts-and-maps.great-chain-being). This source is cited with acknowledgements and thanks.

you know what they're like

"... Racists... looking for ways to excuse what they [say]..." (Harker, J. (2020). *The Guardian*, 11 June, 2020. "Black Lives Matter" risks becoming an empty slogan. It's not enough to defeat racism: www.theguardian.com/commentisfree/2020/jun/11/black-lives-matter-racism-bristol-colston *Quoted with acknowledgements and thanks*).

you know what they're like they're not wanted she said
they should be hassled arrested decanted sifted shifted she said
you know what they're like they come over in shed
loads illicitly shack up in sheds off their heads
I'd need to be dead to be led she said
to bend my knee no I won't she said they're not wanted she said
they spend all day in bed illegally wed
they should be arrested by heads of the Fed
you know what they're like they're not wanted she said
they shouldn't be a dead weight expect to be fed
found an NHS bed when they're incapacita-ted
you know what they're like they should have to mine lead
or unknit knotted thread for worsted instead in sweat shops she said
until they're exhausted or really quite dead
and I'd need to be dead to be led she said
to bend my knee no I won't she said
you know what they're like they're not wanted she said
they should be sifted shifted reported deported departed
they're everywhere she said
in Cheddar Reading Wanstead Stansted Plumstead Oxted Ofsted
Hemel Hempstead Herts and even Hampstead they're hated she said
things have really come to a head don't be misled
I'd need to be dead to be led she said
to bend my knee no I won't she said they're not wanted she said
they should knead their own bread not expect to be fed
by food banks instead not expect to be led
they'll always be hated and baited abated she said
except by Jez who likes reds in his bed it makes me see red
they're not integrated they hate us deflate us slate us she said
I'd need to be dead to be led she said
to bend my knee no I won't she said
you know what they're like they're not wanted she said

Richard Byrt

Statue Outrage *(9ᵗʰ June, 2020)*

Some
people seem
more outraged
 by a bronze
   statue
   which
doesn't breathe
being dragged
 to the ground,
  than the
transportation
of 84,000 enslaved
people,
or a black man,
 George Floyd,
   dying,
   choked
   on the
   street
   at the
   knees
    of
   the
   Police.

Julian Colton

May 2020

This month has been all about breathing;
it's easier in this clear blue air.
We rarely stray from home.
But the ICU wards are filling up
and we all know someone who knows someone else
who will probably be heading there soon.

I turn the TV on and start screaming;
It seems some officers think they *are* the law.
Take your knee off his neck, you racist thugs!
He can't fucking breathe!
How can a man crying for his mother
pose any threat to America?
People are dying in droves!

Mark Connors

Again +

Again
And Again

Anger, Rage, Fury
Protest fuelled by outrage
Pitiless - another life yielded

Slogans, Placards, Voices
On streets and at intersections
Marching from somewhere, to everywhere

Again
Yet Again

Asking questions
Questioning answers
Awaiting action from Power

Blind eyes see nothing
Stopped ears hear nothing
Change too slow, so nothing

Again
Not Again?

John Cooper

Tanka

the traffic cop
doesn't like my attitude
or my skin colour
I don't like the way his hand
hovers on his holster

Tracy Davidson

Burning Churches

Burn down your own church
not that of others.
Set free your symbols,
and let them return.

Allow your altar,
to a neighbour needing a table.
Pass on your candles
to those in a dark home.

Donate your robes
to those cold and shivering.
Melt your statues to gold
for others to spend.

Then from your own ruins,
set out,
with nothing
but a light step

And let the heart be opened,
to the sacred
in all that lives,
outside
these great walls,
of where once stood
such holy ground.

Giles Dawnay

learning to bathe with lava

in their eyes hung a chalkboard
with examples of synonyms for black:
scavenger, stranger, villain,
a diagram of a gaunt crybaby strapped to the back of WHO

they stared me into a skeleton smeared
with a paste of gunpowder & benzene. eyes always
on the look out to detect a flash point
under their *-12°C* words

they called awake:

i. a beast whose claws must rid its body
of the nerves that bellows a siren call at every stolen kiss of a flea

ii. the wish to become an *abiku* whose next adventure
is to wake up in the body of an American boy.
imageries: sight of a shed snake skin on father's fallowed farmland;
a chameleon on dried leaves camouflaging

iii. Google search history: *how to grow asbestos skin*

iv. & to inject pints of blood, from men i know are stones

here is a lyric to my ballad:
if the bullet hole was no period
on the body of Martin Luther, then the story never ended

this is how I bathe with lava;

i duet with the visiting wraith of mother *[we sing the songs*
she sang away the taunting cry of a newborn
man child from father's concubine];

i stand under the seething waterfall,
prefrontal cortex active; there is a smirk on my face.
isn't pain an inept guitarist without
its plectrum of neurons, anterior cingulate cortex?

the rising steam, & smoke of the burnt offering of my being,

like smoking herbs of a rainmaker's invocation,
draws rainclouds in the eyes of God

He weeps dewfall on my bristle hair,
& walks through the vent of my mouth into my belly;
in his mouth, the ripples of an old pond
after *Basho's* frog leaps into it.

Martins Deep

Blackout

Through the keyhole of time
Lives still locked out
Truths spin around lies
Unnoticed whispers quiver
In the suburbs of our minds
Dark shadows curl around
Centuries of sound
Stand up for their rights
A key keeps on turning
A click keeps on repeating
But will the light
Ever be switched on?

Do you hear that sound?
Do you feel
That deep rooted torment
The air lays heavy on the tongue
Muted breath
Generations of injustice
Anguish, fury, pain
Again and again

If the writing is on the wall
Vicious graffiti scrawled
Minds need to shift
Tonight a mother left bereft
Ripped at the seams
She'll never sleep again.
Perceptions need to change

Don't you see she's a city grieving?
Brutal beasts wrapped up as authority
Who gave you the right to end his life?
Such hate behind those violet eyes
Unarmed man calls out
"Please... I can't breathe"

Riots erupt on the streets
A young girl holds up a banner
She cries out

To deaf ears,
"Black lives matter!"

Sara Eliot

To America

I address you, America, from very far away.
Settler-colonial swords in the bowels of earth, god, and nation,
the America I see come into being wears flensed black skins
and with sad red ribbons of resistance
you showed the mauling love of a whitewashed Christ
to the people who lived there long ago – isn't it time
you severed muscle and tendon from riddled bone?
Isn't it time the mini Caesars separated the foundation myth
(careerism through genocide and Jackson's settler jihad) from the nations
underneath, the history of its land, the abysmal lie of its 'Christian soul'?
The bronze bastilles will fall and you will find no veins;
the peoples' hearts will ache, but something new might be seen.
Your narcotic soil, a mess of roots, bleached bone, and ritual vultures
cries out for blood that you must deny, for the greedy Sassenach
and the unbowed Ulster-Scots raised their flag for armies of famine, hangings,
and war (the infant cot of state building), the scalpeens stretched across a bitter
emerald to become the scalps of Navajo, Cherokee and Sioux.
The English bought the heads of Irishmen, then both bought Pequot heads.
The headdress of Puritanism still entrances, and when I look closer each jewel
is dripping with fat, the fat of hearts removed with grim discipline –
this sick inhumanism which eats so politely – anaemic – as the old republic
darkens in poison-tipped rain:
would that republics would perish for their distinctly unrepublican cholesterol
(white cholesterol), so I'll look to Haiti for kindling to reignite the dream of
Paine and Tone.

Blake Everitt

Strength

It wasn't just a seat
Sitting at the back of the bus stood for more than that

It ensured we knew our place
Forever last
It reminded us we would always have to take extra steps
To arrive at the same position
It showed us we weren't part of this society
Literally partitioned

Until Rosa parked herself on that seat and refused to be moved
She could no longer approve the abuse
Decided to dispute
In order to improve
The conditions of our people

They disapproved
Came in suits and boots to accuse her in groups
They felt it was illegal for her to protest their evil

Even though it was peaceful
It was lethal
To try and empower the people

But I wonder how she felt -

Was she willful and determined?
Unafraid of the crosses stood burning?
Was she scared?
Yet overcame the fear to stand for truth
Regardless of the strange fruit hanging from trees by noose

Irrespective of how she felt inside
She decided to take a stand

I can't imagine how much bravery that took
To refuse such commands
Such demands
Going against their plans
I can't imagine but I need to

To gather strength for the people
To speak up for the feeble
Because without me or you there is no breakthrough

I cannot change the world's view of what they deem to be acceptable
But can refuse to be moved
Until the conditions of our people are improved
Instead of turning a blind eye to the truth
So -

which one will you choose?

Ravelle-Sadé Fairman

Black Venus

Jeanne Duval to Charles Baudelaire

I was everything or I was nothing.
I was the over-arching sky, studded
with the beauty of the stars. Else I
was a vessel for the sadness with which
you filled my silence – for the morbid
intensity of your desire to embrace
the infinite (not me), my charms enhanced
by how I fled from you, as if from the worms
of the grave, and from that one limp worm
you had to offer. I was implacable and cruel,
until broken by your worship and its need
to make me exotic. Then when, finally,
you did your best for me, disdain for your
charade of lust could turn, at last, to hate.

Mike Farren

The Ballad of Paulette Wilson

The UK has a cancer which is gnawing at its heart -
the cancer's name is Brexit and it's tearing us apart.
More money for the NHS? No, that was just a laugh;
they're breaking up the service as they terrorise the staff.
Home Office gets the message. The verdict's all too clear:
if you weren't born in Britain, then they don't want you here.
They're not planning for the future with a rational campaign;
they're rounding up the foreigners to put them on a plane.

They pick on Paulette Wilson, down Wolverhampton way,
who gets the dreaded letter that says she cannot stay.
She came here from Jamaica when she was ten years old.
She's 61, a granny, but they've put her life on hold.
Hostile Environment's the plan. It's magic: "Just like that!"
She's always paid her taxes but – shazam! - she's lost her flat.
She spends a week at Yarl's Wood. They send her to Heathrow.
They don't care what she says to them, they mean to make her go.

Her daughter works her socks off, her MP fights the case.
The Home Office is clinging on, they're scared of losing face.
The Guardian writes her story, their readers send support;
solicitors are sure this case will not stand up in court.
She gets a gala evening and a cheque for half a grand
from a load of local poets and a ukulele band.
Eventually the pressure tells, the scandal is a stain
and Paulette gets good news at last – permission to remain.

She wasn't looking for revenge. What mattered to Paulette
was that they say they're sorry, that they viewed this with regret.
Now that this scandal's in the news, they'll want the slate wiped clean.
She used to work in Parliament with staff from the canteen
but suddenly she's back there, on Tuesday, first of May,
where Caroline Nokes, Home Office, has stuff she needs to say:
"To Mrs. Wilson, specially…" - she looks her in the eyes –
"You suffered from our policies. I must apologise."
Recommendations were ignored. So many people wait
for compensation that is due; for Paulette it's too late.
She was bright and energetic but they tore her life apart
and now, at 64, she's died. The battle broke her heart.
She gets a Covid funeral, just twenty folk inside

but there's hundreds in the car park, they're applauding her with pride.
When governments abuse their power, we have to set them right
and she's the Windrush champion who has taught us how to fight.

Paul Francis

Shackles

Chain link: Make LEGAL immigrants   ILLEGAL
Chain link: Shame us into thinking we don't belong here
Chain link: Use your vans to scare us of breathing
Chain link: Your words fill your society with fear
Chain link: Tell them, we're here to steal   what you took
Chain link: Create a country high on fear
Chain link: Put pen to paper to keep us hooked
Chain link: Tell the landlord he can no longer house us there
Chain link: Let the employer know we're no longer employable
Chain link: All the taxes we've paid can't help us now
Chain link: No money to pay a lawyer to sort this shit out
Chain link: Fuck! Even the GP is policing us now
Chain link: You don't turn up to court or forget why you're there
Chain link: More time wasted, we're stuck in your engineered
                hole of despair
Chain link: If we don't report, we're told "You may face penalties"
Chain link: And jailed in detention indefinitely
Chain link: While there you treat us like scum
Chain link: You rape us, sexually abuse us, use your words
                to break us down
Chain link: Using us as slave labour paying an hour for a pound
Chain link: Did you investigate – what became of that?
Chain link: SUICIDES in detention
Chain link: You mentally broke them down
Chain link: Hooray! You say, one less, the numbers going down
Chain link: When we're sick, you say, "You faking it"
Chain link: You threaten to handcuff us to make us walk like penguins
Chain link: If we don't die five days later
Chain link: No point going to the hospital
Chain link: They will let us die!
Chain link: Conscience filed away in their crackdown of 'The Other'
Chain link: Frustrated and sick exactly where you want us
Chain link: So tired…
Chain link:
Chain link:

Michelle Fuller

Endnote:
1. "The hostile environment is a sprawling web of immigration controls embedded in the heart of our public services and communities. The Government requires

employers, landlords, private sector workers, NHS staff and other public servants to check a person's immigration status before they can offer them a job, housing, healthcare or other support." *A Guide To The Hostile Environment*, edited by Liberty.

2. Woman accused of faking illness to avoid UK deportation died five days later.

South African Nancy Motsamai collapsed while being escorted through Heathrow airport.

"An immigration official at the airport accused Nancy of faking her collapse to avoid being put on a plane," her husband said. "He told Nancy that he would handcuff her hands and feet and make her walk to the plane like a penguin..." *The Guardian*

Necessary Evil

Forced entry into her Garden of Eden – her tree of life raped of its
knowledge of good…

The pull at her nipple was not from the mouth of her own – they stole her
nutrients. Her roots and seedlings sold at market for profit – to feed their
offspring.

Proud to take ownership of the necessary wealth piled up from their
malevolence.

But don't you dare, speak truth of their evil buried deep in souls and soil
and seas. Trauma exposed to open-air, sailing through nostrils and blood
streams – lodged in lungs. You would be considered ungrateful – told to
get over it.

Michelle Fuller

Hostile

How would you have this end?
When that mummy, that daddy,
that little boy and girl,
no longer soft-skinned humans,

are now subsumed in a mass,
swarming, amorphous; labels
hanging off their threadbare
clothes: *Rats! Vermin!*

Where would you draw a line?
How far do we speed sightless
down this fairground corkscrew?
Scream if you want to go faster.

How snugly do you fit within
your own snow white Utopia?
How deep do your roots reach
in this shifting Anglo soil?

How blanched is your face
at the notion of your own child
all gasped out and pink in some
gas chamber of your dreams?

When will you breakdown,
unlock your jaildoor arms
and wrap them fast around
a pair of heaving shoulders
from the same planet as you?

Harry Gallagher

Sunday Read, Cill Rialaig

A glossy picture of Rubaya.
just a place where miners toil for pence;
they dig in descending steps
down to Congo's brown-red core,
each step is eight foot long by eight foot wide
by nine foot deep (this last dimension
decreasing the chances of decapitation);
their quarry coltan, a rare commodity used in
mobile phones and computers;
its high market value lures the usual jackals:
the multinationals, other criminal gangs,
corrupt politicians, fat cats,
each comfortable with their greed,
each steadfast in their right to make slaves of others.

But what of us, the workers, the drones,
Capital's little helpers, the oilers of its grinding wheels?
What of us, the teachers of false values,
too scared to say when enough is enough;
false preachers of acceptance
too snug to say that This is wrong;
pseudo Coms and cuter Cons
debating shades of pink and blue
at overladen tables;
politics's scum still plucking the poorest
to feather their own soft-centred nests?

But what of us, the locust tribe
devouring all before us,
leaving nothing in our wake? What of us.
consumers of the latest fad,
the brands, the trinkets, the tosh,
bloodied by lost fingers of some child slave in Bangladesh,
or the last polluted gasp of a peasant in China or India,
or the soil-stenched sweat of an African miner?
What of us? Do we care? Do we care at all?
Driven by our greed, surrounded by our clutter,
do we count the cost to our fellow men?
Do we rate them above our poodles?

Are we not, all of us, jackals at heart,
some slightly uncomfortable?

Mike Gallagher

No signal

The mobile buzzes, buzzes,
startles, allows only hard
choices, old unreachable contacts,

displays a flecked rainbow
of a starling
singing in an odd dialect.

I hear the easy clatter of trains
passing but a clear signal
does not arrive, and I wait

at the window as if a dual sim
transfers the data of marshes
where unseen egrets visit.

Moira Garland

A discovery of witches

The Pendle Witches a fable
until on a tour of Lancaster Castle I look
in the cell where those women were held
for real.

Evil flesh and blood,
deformities, and *desiccated crones'* grim
wickedness turning beer sour, murder,
with mysterious powers without power
to stop their own demise at Gallows Hill
named after these *daemons* still,
women supposed to be
easily deceived, of slippery tongue
who *receive impressions from the devil.*

James' *Daemonologie*, Roger Nowel JP,
names of the men possessed of powers-that-be
foretold the spells of orange suits
waterboard duckings
play/ed divide and rule with
family feuds
forbidden faiths

just as children walking home from school
where trees hide a derelict house, a weed high garden,
on the opposite side of the road,
whisper each other a tale
'that's where the witch lives'
dare not let out a breath,
are kept in check.

Moira Garland

Italicised words are from King James' *Daemonologie* (1597).

Roger Nowell JP was the prosecutor and magistrate responsible for collecting the
various statements and confessions from the accused, who were then tried at
Lancaster assizes in 1612.

Livingstone's End

Hallucinations take him back
to cold wet Scottish dawns,
to tumbling tenement stairways,
      slaving twelve-hour days
in the spinning factory's din - another
cotton thread to tie among the looms.

Malaria shakes his bones at Inlala.
Pneumonia and cholera embrace him,
      bites raise ulcers on his feet.
His hut is restless, dark with dreams
of John, evangelising father;
      each knock and clatter of the mill.
He shifts his lion-damaged arm.
Once-nimble fingers pluck at cloth.
      So close to death he must depend
on Arab merchants he despises,
tells them he was once a slave of trade.

His vision was of medicine and mission
but commerce won't help Africa,
      won't lift oppression's knee.
      From granite streets to humid forests,
he failed every river, village, rapids, fall.

Kathy Gee

Breathe
after George Floyd

Glittering pink paper confettis
to the floor as I open my presents.
The usual collection of cards
are displayed on the window sill.
I'm sitting under a safe blue sky
and the old sun keeps me company as usual.
The Earth's beautiful spin is particularly lazy today.
I breathe in and my lungs don't know they are lucky.

4000 miles away, George,
cheek pressed to concrete,
takes a breath, inhales the entire street
until a police officer kneels on his neck.
The Earth spins faster and falls off its axis.

Mama

                    Someone's son begs for his mother,

Everything hurts

                    crying into hot tarmac under the unforgiving sky,

I can't breathe

                    his unlucky lungs.

Deep breath,
make a wish,
keep the wish close.
I blow out the candles,
create tiny ghosts
that will be remembered.

Rachel Glass

52

Trials of a Calabash Bowl

This heirloom has moved
Several times from one city to another,
while the layer beneath the sky watched

and the gods in front of the clouds watched
its edges and how they break, when cold
hands of strangers prod rough
and the cracking sound the weather
and its elements make,
when rainstorm tries to wash precious art.

Listen. This calabash has already been
on the dangerous daring treetop of palm wine trees,
lived in the softness of cotton
stalks, stalking
the roughness of old country lanes
and their dead-end corners.

Hear. This piece of inheritance has tasted
Salty water
Held rocks
and now holds today's water
drawn from a new spring.

Lind Grant-Oyeye

Dare to Cross

you stood, blair,
white against white

till, in this land growing brown,
you were, by white,

struck white

who was blair peach,
we ask the children in blair peach school

and they do not know
the winners of the blair peach award

have never read the lyrics of ralph mctell
never sighted the radiance of peach

crossing the boundary
between new zealand and this country

crossing the boundary between this
world and the next

did you glimpse why the emperor zhu houcon
yellowed china by the flames

greying his own navy
or why the tokugawa iemitsu

bloodied his own people
did you suddenly spot why argentina declined

from being the richest country in the world
did you foresee russia closing under putin

india under modi
america under trump

england ruled by the people you resisted

they want to freeze
what you were struggling to keep flowing

you lost colour
we gained

so we dare to cross the boundary
take the blair as our own

we breathe peach air
peach blood flows in our veins

we blare, glare, flare

Peach.

Prabhu S. Guptara

This poem is written in memory of Blair Peach, the New Zealander who was killed by members of the SPG (a specialist unit at that time in the Metropolitan Police Force) during an anti-racism demonstration in Southall, in April 1979. Public dismay at the killing, as well as police cover-ups following that for several years (combined with other contributory factors) led to the 1971 Brixton riot, and to the Public Inquiry by Lord Scarman, with consequent changes in the law. A school in Southall is named after Peach, the National Union Teachers has since 2010 given the Blair Peach Award each year to recognise work on equality and diversity, *One For Blair* (anthology of poems) was edited by Chris Searle (1989), *The 2-Tone Story* album is dedicated to Peach's memory, and there are many others who wish to keep Peach's legacy from being extinguished. The fresh outburst of anger occasioned by the murder of George Floyd is a good time to remember the long struggle against police killings of Black people and of those who have supported the struggle for racial justice.

Please note that "blair" is Scots for "field"

The caged bird

The caged bird
Is beautiful and black
flutters her wings

She still sings
The caged bird
Fights slumber at night
So she can breathe and write
Writes page after page

Yes she still sings
The caged bird
Soars the midnight sky
When she writes words into her dreams
Paints the sky a red dye

Yes she still sings
The caged bird
Marches the streets
For
Black lives matter
Hoping just hoping
That for justice
Truth and solidarity will meet

I 've been waiting
With my heart
Marching to the sun
Burdened my heavy shoulders
Constantly looking back
Life is a survival run
Yet my beauty
I have been told to hide and shun
But I own my colour my skin
I own the song
that resonates
my soul
within

Nusrat M Haider

Ma'ati

… while that owl in the tree
is hooting blissfully,
to the sound of
Gil Scott-Heron's B Movie,
Fabian's Prophecy,
Get up! Stand up! Bob Marley,
that is playing from the stereo
of apartment Number 3
since last Tuesday morning, at 6.30...

downstairs

Ma'ati tries to practice her Tai Chi.
Calls Eshaye! Fi di whole a wi,
and raises up her arms
in the name of Justice and Peace!
　　A breath　　*says her name*
breathes out　　lights a candle...
stands from her knees,
lifts up her head with dignity

grabs her covid mask,
her lunch box, her flask,
then out, and into the city…

Jean Hall

The B Side

Brutality and bias both begin
with the letter b,
                    like banned,
bigot, baton, bled, bleed
bleeding red on the pavement
again,
bent by beliefs
of the unbending.

Look
        at first-world banana-republics
lean on the necks of those they count as
'under',
            tread them for a cash crop
to the credit of those that dictate
the value placed on a human head.

Hear
        the blue blues butterfly-heartache,
bone-weary with building bridges
brought to nothing, nothing, no thing
over rivers of life every bit as bright
as any other body of water.

Touch
        the beauty.

Say
        what you see in the brightness
of a soul rising, despite,
in spite of.

Smell
        the brazen goodness.

Bear
        the names of those
stained without cause, and

feel
    their breeze fill your sails and theirs
to carry you together
to the other side
where we could not get to a-
part.

Roger Hare

What matters

I love black people.
But that doesn't matter, because like the mother, father, brother,
sister, spouse or friend that does nothing to heal a wound of the other,
they have a title and they do nothing that title entails.
That concept is abstract and that love is cold.

I have black people in my family.
But that doesn't matter, if systematic, racial prejudice runs free
in high up institutions, education, government, art, and every other sector
and does not get challenged by my life.
That concept is abstract and that love is cold.

I am not racist.
But that does not matter, if I alone say nothing, see no privilege
and see a silent belief system as a complete redemption of generations
of unspeakable, unthinkable, barbaric, unforgivable, inhuman abuse against
another.
That concept is abstract and that love is cold.

All lives matter.
But that doesn't matter, if one group under that rubric has been
discounted, displaced, with inequality beyond words, until this
very day, all day, everyday, to a disproportionate and indistinguishable
level.
That concept is abstract and that love is cold.

Black lives matter.

Samantha Harper-Robins

And suddenly air

And in that moment
as they hauled his statue down

to roll it clanking to the quay
drown it in the Reach

we grasped the enormity of a story
come full circle

a black knee
pressed to the slaver's neck

and suddenly
air

where all our lives
stood cruelty, shame.

Deborah Harvey

On 7th June 2020, after decades of failed attempts to get the statue of slave trader Edward Colston either removed from Bristol city centre or put into historical context, protestors on the Black Lives Matter demonstration dragged it from its plinth and dumped it in the city's Floating Harbour.

Up the Street

The barber shops. One for the white folks. One
for the jews. The afro place where they can actually cut
black hair. The punks DI, we share bottles of dye

over cans of Red Stripe in our grimy bathroom. The neon green.
The pink. The bleached with Domestos, stuck up
with wood glue. The rockers. The rastas. The dreadlocks.

The skinheads. The hooligans, ready to string up the first face
that doesn't fit. The us and them, our standards marking out
battle lines. That infamous confrontation of Cable Street in 1936.

The workers. The antifascists. The peace lovers. The paper passed
from hand to hand, that rally cry. *'No pasarán!'* The blackshirts.
The boot tread. The parade that comes up against barricades.

The pallets. The abandoned trams. The upholstered chair -
a gold and green brocade defender. A witness from a window
sees a young man taken out by the sharp crack of a policeman's

black baton. He falls, his face a mask of outrage. They move in.
Blood trickles from his forehead. A white faced woman behind him
throws up her arm, covers her eyes. The defence. The rocks,

chair legs, rotten veg. Throwing missiles. 7000 policemen
and 3000 fascists. The posters. The headlines. FASCISM CAN
AND WILL WIN BRITAIN. The retaliation. 85 arrests, only six

of the bastards among them. The charges. Insulting words.
Obstructing police. Wilful damage. Assault. Grievous bodily harm.
Damage to police clothing. The brave. The savage. The red flag.

Billy Bragg sings on the radio and Yusuf dusts the short blond hairs
from his customer's neck, inspects his work. The towel.
The scissors. The razor. The music. The silence.
The chatter from the street in Whitechapel, no two accents the same.
The Times shouts FIRMS MUST LIST FOREIGN WORKERS.
Across London, a mausoleum looms against the skyline.

The artist. The OAP dancer. The schoolgirl just starting her A levels.

The protests. The headlines. The grief. The silence.   The photos,
people of colour smiling out at us from the front pages.

The corner shop selling Heinz tomato soup and an exhaustive
range of spices. The bustle. The litter. The ringing of the bell. The idle
chat over change, receipt. The community park, alive with groups

chatting, drinking, laughing. The benches. I swing and shout.
The roundabout. The flowerbeds, bright with tulips; red, yellow, pink.
The pigeons. The neon green of the ring-necked parakeets.

Jem Henderson

How to Get Rid of Christopher Columbus

Don't get photographed presenting your
two thousand names to the Mayor,
looking as if you're graduating
with a qualification you'll never use.
Don't ask the Church of Ireland or National Council
for the Advancement of Concerned People
to intervene.

Do it yourself.
But not explosives, no.
There's always a mostly innocent
retired car park attendant with a limp
(or some such) passing at the exact moment.
He retired five years ago
but because of the limp
was still on his way home.
And now he's in small pieces
or, even worse,
one piece;
and you're the reason
he has that stutter
when the journalist talks to him
on the every o'clock news.

Nothing like a spot of terrorism
gone amiss
to make all that racism, pillage, and slicing
off most of a native's thigh
just to test your blades
or a child's hand
because their parents wouldn't cooperate
with what was
an honest attempt to improve them
seem civilised in comparison.

Arm yourself with
no mere plinkety chisel
but mallet, kango hammer,
a couple of the like-minded,
and high vis jackets marked

'City Council' or 'Irish Water'
and present the slow citizenry
with the fact
of his stone tribute
in the sea.

Kevin Higgins

The UK is Not Innocent

We are quick
to point the finger

at the US
as an example

of the most heinous
anti-black racism

that has taken place
for over 400 years

but the UK is
perhaps worse

racism here is
a leopard concealing
itself in tall grass

disguised
as ignorance or
heedful looks
at black men

but black people have
still died
in police custody
here

Sarah Reed
Mark Duggan
Sheku Bayoh
Christopher Alder
Leon Patterson
Cynthia Jarrett
Sean Rigg

These souls
are just a few of many

So don't tell me *the UK is innocent.*
It's not.

Arun Jeetoo

police

police	my body
police	my language
police	my sexuality
police	my healthcare
police	my education
police	my occupation
police	my ancestors
police	my generation
police	my civil rights.

Arun Jeetoo

bougainvillaea reminds her of home
the pink petals
warm
the colour of human flesh
scatter the sandy streets
crinkling
crushing
under the simmering sun
like the dreams
of the youth
she stitches to her skin
as they stare at the barrel end of a loaded gun

she sews their hopes with her happiness
weaves war with wishes
wonders
if the flag she's shouldering
drips blood

Hamdi Khalif

Cobalt in Congo

every cloud is pregnant with storm and thunder
shells crack in zig-zags
C the sections that intersect:

a neon flash captures yet another violent scene,
transforming involuntary martyrs with their final plea
into moving imagery,

were they told as their last breath left
that the gods would use their death
transforming their souls into pixels, send
them into digital limbo then
hope for the best - for humanity to wake up in protest

on display, another black life is slayed
the force of Thor's hammer could not compare
to our battleaxe rage
to the force of our prayers
to the punch of every fist raised
electrocuting the skies
with
knuckles clenched tight
around smartphones, documenting
from as many angles possible

underwater in the deepest shades of blue
whales stay singing funeral songs
they lead you to lands of coco and requiem

here there are spirits waiting to kiss you
on both cheeks,
 'Welcome'

foreign, but not quite estranged
with
knuckles clenched tight
around shovels as they dig for lithium
how the colonial system
is still ingrained and keeps them
carving out what could be their grave

for less than a dollar as daily wage,

kids raising their hands, not in class
but in offering
of minerals fueling global movement
online, press play
they have paved the way
for us to

click, share, post, forget
click, share, post, forget

our awareness is raised as facebook feeds
not their bellies
but our morbid curiosity

the WorldWideWeb seeks
out what bleeds fresh
minds are fed,
graphic content lands heavy,
buries itself into your chest
tag,
discuss,
stream, live

Love,
look closely through fish eyes

they are hyper sensitive to polarised light
look, hear, taste
their salt when they cry

all black lives are bound
together in struggle and in spite
of it
together we rise

Kihwa-Endale

Behind all Fear is Freedom

Behind all fear is freedom -
there is no other way -
to overcome hardship in your life -
face it every day.

There is no use avoiding
the reality inside.
Running away one only finds
there is no place to hide.

There is no shame in failing -
when trying so hard to do.
Victory comes to the heart
that makes its dreams come true.

So face your fears with courage -
conquer them one by one.
It is the price the soul must pay
to bask in freedom's sun.

Tom Krause

Darnella's Duty

Darnella Frazier is the brave young woman who filmed the murder of George Floyd on May 25, 2020

How does it feel to be 17,
and just want to hold your life in your
glistening palm, go to the corner
and buy a sparkling water to quench
a parched mouth that longs to sing?

How does it feel to witness
a purpose too cruel
for all your 17 rotations
around a sun you only want to bask in?

How does it feel to beg a name,
witness a life breaking,
while your opened ebony eyes,
see loss and corruption corralled
to the borderless sky?

And, how does the humid wind feel
as you watch it carry one man's life
to a crevice where only the wind can go?

Laurie Kuntz

Dear Vallejo

Your people are crying out to you for help,
demanding an end to the violence,
yet you do not truly hear them
if your response is tear gas and guns.

If a man has a hammer and you see a gun,
then you need to get your eyes checked.
If you think people should die over property,
then you need to get your heart checked.

If you're more offended by curse words
than the death of your neighbors,
then you need to check your morality.

Your people need compassion not force,
real solidarity not empty platitudes,
social change not more of the same,
due process not more executions,
redemption not discrimination.

Join the chorus whose tune is justice.
It is growing louder and louder by the day.

D.L. Lang

Milton-on-the-Hill

And the man spied on the bridal path,
shimmering, vaporous, slow in gait
like a predator through grass, is black.
Parents waiting at the school gate
ask, *Does he wear a backpack?*

Our village is tasked with isolation
like an open wound wary of infection.
A Jamaican lived here for a season,
drank in the pub with his white wife's son.
Are you visiting? we asked.

Our childminder is on the back lane
when the man falls in step, asks her name.
He is a carer for a chronic smoker
in Norden Heath. Going for a walk
is the only way he can breathe.

Charles G Lauder, Jr

Mordor over the Shire any day

Sometimes you have to go to
Mordor, not the shire,
to witness your mind change
And feel connected

Love and sadness for your city (Santa Monica)
also activates when it becomes Gotham City.
Merch, paper shreds in alleyways triumphant.
Ground zero for finding accomplishment.
And yet I get it.
Connectivity and values aren't trickling in America
or… you tell me

There's many views and angles to this.
A thirst for understanding.
7-Eleven was conveniently wedged open
for a water break if I needed it

Adriano Timoteo Llosa

Yaa Asantewaa

Could I have passed through it all, the stories would range
In patterns different to those the world inherits;
And phrases like this, which prevented any change -
The European nations carved up Africa -
Would have been consigned to the dustbin of histories.

But I died in exile, with fifteen close advisers;
Yaa Asantewaa, who should have lived forever
A woman who led the Asante against an Empire,
A Queen who provoked her people to rebellion:
History might have been changed, and the Empire undone.

Now only my name lives, endures in you, the beholder,
Who carry it in the casket of your black knowledge.

First, some events and names: the Atlantic trade in slaves
Erasing the image and story of black St Maurice.
Yet there long remained, in the heart of Africa,
A stone-built city, not governed by race or ethnicity,
But by passion and pride, a challenge to later oppression.

All this might have been in my head when I rose up.
But it was not. There were issues in black and white.
Thereafter, when I was gone, then the Golden Stool
Resisted like sunlight the British Governor-general.
Strange that the power of things can be greater than bullets.

Easy to understand why soldiers might believe
That to touch a sacred icon will give protection.
Or to hear the Words of belief and inspiration
Will enable the poor to thrive, and the dead to rise:

Montu mo danta mma me na monnye ne tam.

And yet I once lived; now live in commemoration,
As I did when I gave my speech to fellow Asante,
Appealing to the legends from which they had sprung.
That Time was lost. Even now we have scarcely begun.
Though no-one remembers Frederick Mitchell Hodgson!

Rob Lowe

77

Any Bus Stop In England
(In memory of Stephen Lawrence)

He was one,
they were more.
He is gone,
they are above the law.
Like the bus that didn't come,
his journey was over before it had barely begun.

They walk,
he has fallen.
They laugh and talk,
his voice has been stolen.
Like the bus doors that did not open,
justice stays closed and unspoken.

They are free,
living in a world that allows this to be.
Unquestioned by friends and family
in a system that allows complicity.
Like some bus of old, that allowed segregation,
not recognising we all deserve the same destination.

Living goes on,
in a world of different skin.
His life briefly shone,
remembered as a beautiful thing.
Change takes so long,
but change we have to bring.
Until the hatred is gone.
Like the bus that doesn't come,
next time it might be your son.

Paul Lyalls

Only Black in Summer

Here
I am only black
In summer
When the sun
Kisses my skin
Back to the darkness
Of a tropical youth
And winter's blanch
Is lifted.
Then
There are fewer smiles
More suspicious looks
Store clerks lingering
Awkwardly at nearby shelves
Eyes sliding over face
And bags
And curious eyes

Try to decide
What box I fit in
What hole I came from.
Always
I walk between
Us and them
Till winter takes the sun
And pales my skin
And I fade
Into the background
Again and
Looking differently
Am looked at
Differently.

Margaret Mair

Rottnest Island Quokkas

Named 'Rat's Nest' in 1696 by Dutch explorers after the quokka
population that lives there, Rottnest Island is a tourist haven in Western
Australia. It was for a long period a prison for aboriginal Australians and
one of the biggest death-in-custody sites in Australia.

The island is sun-cream and golden surface,
chocolate ice-cream and parasols and quokkas,

quokkas, perfect selfie-fodder:
the cutest, cat-sized rat-kangaroos

with winsome faces, poised front paws,
rounded ears and perpetual smiles.

He crouches at a distance, waits for his moment.
She's busy, combing the sedge for samphire.

He could lure her with a piece of doughnut and sugar,
but it's not allowed. So he keeps still,

sinks forward, ear to the ground with his camera.
Sudden silence. He cannot hear the chatter

from the villas, the raucous shouts of surfers.
Nothing. As if the earth is distilled to its secrets,

the voices that were never allowed to speak in life
and now cannot, leaving just the quietness of quokkas.

She scampers up eventually, and he can't help himself.
He reaches and manages to *stroke a quokka.*

Her fur is coarse. It always looks soft on Twitter.
She wriggles away but he gets his shot

and follows. He pinches a piece of samphire
and tastes the straight-tipped stalk; the salt

catches him off-guard and jars
with the chocolate ice-cream he enjoyed earlier.

He walks away and ends the day with a bathe,
consoling himself that *all lives matter*,

it was *all in the past,* and at least *I don't see colour.*
He sleeps to the sound of the island's sighs,

the fairy terns and silver gulls and sandpipers.
We'll never know what happened in his dreams

but the next day he doesn't share the picture.

Isabella Mead

House against house

Why deny this seed was brought by others,
        germinated in religion and in a single language,
instilled the colour of skin, if it is like our land
        it had to bleach to the paleness of bones.

Land is land and never denies welcome
        It opened its pores, let that root grow,
even though it later told them 'leave,' they didn´t
        understand its languages, they stayed and partied,

their crucifixes still speak, dictate commandments
        as they did at first with slavery and *encomienda*.
Supposedly they left, yes they left us the virtue of the believer,
        the consolations of a god who didn´t understand our people.

Salvation was a perfect plan, while ships
        set sail with gold, the friars delivered prayers.
With what face they said 'it is the will of the Lord',
        with what face they lied in the name of God.

The natives believed, certainly, the natives fell,
        and those others boast that they left us a legacy
to be proud of because they donated their genes,
        the Church and a language. 'What would have become of you

without our golden arrival, you would have no celebrations
        of the Way of the Cross, the bullring and the Day of the Race,'
as if they were a big deal. And the worst is, after
        five centuries the seed lingers in the heads of those at home

who judge by the colour of complexion
        dreaming of resembling they who arrived, their lighter appearance.
If we wanted to see, we would know the roots of hatred
        grow by not accepting what one is.

Lester Gómez Medina

No More Silence

I write because I am sad
I write because I can no longer be silent
I am choking
It hurts
All the pain

I am weary
I am overwhelmed
I can't breathe

"It's just the black men," they say.
"No one kills the women!"

How can you not see?

Killing my husband
Killing my daughter
Killing my neighbour
Killing my voice
You have killed me

Your feigned ignorance
Your denial
You shatter every piece of me
Every day
We can't breathe

Today I choose to speak
You have kept me in bondage for too long
"Angry black woman," you call me

Killing my voice

I deserve to be angry.
Angry about lost lives,
Lost opportunities
Lost dreams and broken promises

You are strangling me
I can't breathe!

Maureen Mguni

Incident

I've come to see what remains of my son
before they wash the pavement.

There are flowers sticking out of a fence
where strangers have paid tribute –

dying leaves: a golden mass of light
still in their plastic.

As I approach the concrete melted into blood
a yellow-blue board screams:

Fatal Gang In Confidence

I step away from the cracks and see the guts
have said too much, each drop a part of him I knew:

the sheet where he was born

a nose bleed on a white, white shirt

outline of a boy with three knife wounds.

Why is it my child locked in an airless box
and not that man, frowning in his car?

Or her, a girl I do not know
and did not push into this world?

My blood has fallen on the ground.
I am the blood torn from his heart.

These strangers want to help me stand
but where he fell, this pavement
frames me gentle enough.

Jenny Mitchell

Black Men Should Wear Colour

For my brother

I mean an orange coat,
sunlight dripping down the sleeves.

A yellow shirt to clash with bright blue trousers –
taking inspiration from the most translucent sea.

Pink leather shoes. Fuchsias might be best
to contrast with brown skin.

Red socks should add some warmth,
so long as they're the only flames to ever touch your feet.

A tie could be mistaken for a noose,
unless you choose a rainbow swirling on your chest.

It will help to show the heart
has all the colours in the world.

Walk down any street with head held high.
I will wave my colours back and we'll both be safe.

Jenny Mitchell

Geometry

Limbs wrenched at obtuse
angles, he estimates the radius
of a fist. All questions are
unintelligible; each transversal
line intersecting with ignorance,
as deadly as a knee to the neck.
Silence is an unanswered question,

like inequality is an unexamined
concept: one thousand, seven
hundred and forty-one more have
died without justice. Find X if Y is
police brutality; find X if Y is in-
humanity; find X if Y is a man crushed
beneath the heel of state-sanctioned

murder. There will be no more of this.
Throw away these textbook deceptions.
Unbalanced equations don't solve
themselves, just like unaccountable
institutions don't police themselves.
This is when things change. Because
nothing is neutral. Not even geometry.

Leanne Moden

Breathe

Oh sweet Jesus
what more can one man do than cry out
in plain English, in desperation –
help me, I can't breathe
and what shall we do then?

Let him breathe? Let him live?
Only that? And if it was your father,
your grandfather, your neighbour
being wheeled away to a ventilator,
crying out from the Covid ward
help me, I can't breathe...
what then?

What if the cries were from somewhere else,
somewhere far or different or where the law alters
according to whose knee is on whose neck
yet still the rule of nature applies –
a man must breathe or else he dies.

Or from a place where pleading is still heard
even when the words aren't understood.
Ya 'iilhi, Bana yardım edin! Ó édes Jezus
have mercy on me,
I can't breathe.

Asem, oddech, hūxī, sum, anáil, respiração
help me
help me
sweet Jesus
I'm only a man, like you.
When will we learn to
separate sin from suffering?

Take your knee off my neck
and kneel on the ground instead.
Put your hands together in prayer,
raise your arms to the sky
and fill your lungs with air.
Breathe.

Cheryl Moskowitz

When

And when the children say
we remember it like it was yesterday
       11-year-old Sanna whose mum held on
       to her box of tinned sardines
       and bag of white rice
       like she used to hold on to Sanna
       saying *you are the most*
       precious, you are all I have
then they have grown too old too soon.

And when those who are already old say
2 metres feels like 2,000 miles away
       82-year-old Clara still shielding
       somewhere in Sheffield can't
       remember the name
       of the granddaughter
       in the photograph she's holding
       or where the cat food is stored
then we have all been forgotten.

And when death tolls in Durban
still rise like Mississippi floodwater
       and Mr. Joseph calls out to
       the neighbour he's never met,
       from the top floor window
       of his home, *now we're all*
       together in the Superdome
       not prisoners but not free either
then there is no war and nothing to be won.

Cheryl Moskowitz

What The Children Drew

They ran from one Sudan into
another and inside the camp
the adults said they should draw pictures
so they drew small objects
in a sky - a skipping girl,
a snake curled round a tree,
a plane that spat out bullets
while it dropped its bombs, huts
unhit so far, a football goal.
The blank white space between
the objects was a silent
scream they'd often heard
but hadn't drawn on yet.

Hubert Moore

Three Hours

We went to the beach today.
The paper says that every day
two people in Detention Centres
end their lives. The sea
was utterly placid, its waves
could hardly rise enough to fall.
You couldn't miss its power,
how the incoming tide
had thrown a ridge of pebbles
up along the shore. We stayed
three hours on the beach
while inland, in the same land
as the tide was going out,
at Colnbrook, Harmondsworth, etc
0.25 Immigration Detainees
killed themselves on average.

Hubert Moore

God I Love My Son

God I love my son. *WaChiuta mwana wane nkhumutemwa.*
WaChiuta I love my son. I had my son when I was still a teenager
back then kukaya ku Malawi.
I remember the day I first entered Chatinkha labour ward that year.
I remember that month, that day. I remember that night.
It was 3:50AM that my son showed up.
He was cute and he still is now.
WaChiuta I love my son.

I remember the first time he suckled my breasts.
I smiled.
And that will forever stay with me.
Children are a blessing so they say.
I agree I am blessed.
With my son, we grew together, and were closely knitted together.
WaChiuta I love my son. *God I love my son.*

My son always knew what I was thinking by just looking in my eye.
All those are just memories now.
I feel incomplete.
He sends me photos we took together but that is not enough for me.
I feel empty.
That connection no longer exists.
My son ali ku Malawi while I live here in the UK.
WaChiuta I love my son.

God I love my son.
The tagline and status that I often use.
It is my way of testifying to God that
no matter the feelings my son may have,
No matter how anyone else may judge me for what has happened in my life
I will forever love my son.
Like a rock I will stand with my son.
Nothing has or will change that part of me for him.
God I love my son.

WaChiuta I love my son.
It is an affirmation.
It is a promise.
It is a declaration.

I miss my son and I know he misses me too.
We miss each other.
WaChiuta I love my son.

Sometimes we cry together on the phone.
We console each other.
Believing that one day our story will change.
God I love my son.

WaChiuta I love my son is a protest to show that whatever barriers that
have been mounted between us, my heart is always with him.

God I love my son is a status that comes from the deepest part of my heart.
I know I have failed him but it stands:
God I love my son. *WaChiuta mwana wane nkhumutemwa.*

Loraine Masiya Mponela

Shoes at the gate

At the river,
you drink to friends lost.
Passports are not trophies.
Shoes at the gate are not talismans.
Questions are markers of struggles seen
but not understood, not engaged with
because other things
had to be done first.
Questions are promises made
that can no longer be kept.

Ambrose Musiyiwa

Black Boys

Black boys shouldn't be out tonight.
Black men, maybe, only if they want to die.

I tell him not to take my son with him,
"Go to the protest alone."

He says my son must know the truth
and that I can't hide him forever.

I win the battle tonight,
and in twelve blankets I will shelter you.
In twelve prayers I will cover you,
for I know, I won't hide you forever.
your daddy will be back,
and the world will be waiting,
so will I.

Linda Nabasa

Of The Times

The sign said: STOP
　But we flatly refused.
　Out in bloom, fresh out the womb
　American Dreamin'.

The sign said: DON'T WALK
　But we marched on, didn't we?
　Defying laws that held us down,
　on some anti-gravity shit.

The sign said: NO LOITERING
　But we had nowhere else to play.
　So we hooped with hollowed milk crates
　before the sun went missing.

The sign said: SWIM AT YOUR OWN RISK
　But drowned dreams kept washing up.
　And they don't make life preservers
　in our size. Or color.

The sign said: NOT A THROUGH STREET
　But how many learned that the hard way?
　On corners we learn to ask for a light
　before directions, straight up.

The sign said: ROAD WORK AHEAD
　But what about inside? Tell me: Who
　do we call to fix the sinkholes in our souls--
　like a thousand mouths agape.

The sign said: NO SMOKING
　But guns can't read.

The sign said: STOP
　But we didn't see the word; only red.
　And if you squint, the bloom of blood
　on the concrete looks just
　　like roses.

Russell Nichols

The Rights of One

Hatred is a pregnant mother too
and I have become a tiny man
but not so small hatred gets anything
over on me, just one who is able
to love, one who recalls his mother
long after she was pregnant with
a baby boy who grew to take a stand,
who knew eventually how to stand
against hatred, especially the kind
he felt should be called subtle,
the worse kind of hatred, able to trick
the tricksters, able to take away a
simple ability to love, meant to be
a beginning for the rights of one, a
chance to grow out of this tiny body
and stand up to any lies & lures
by the liar sent & paid to steal
the rights of One, to say where he wants
to call home, a new home if he must,
someplace he like I would prefer,
after surviving the last put down.

2.

Theft is a fertile young father even,
and I become a tinier kind of man
with a big pen ready to run out of ink,
a reason to consider the stupid man
isn't anyone I want close to it,
it being all about a man ready
to leave a place hatred takes down
by the insistence of war & poverty,
& disease & torture & politicians.
All enough for the cowards, the
annoying upstarts, a young man
eager to misunderstand what the
rights of One will cause, will allow

the poet to make with proper words,
another tiny man growing tinier as
our time becomes just one day I
will again take a stand beside
all those coming to our Canada,
coming to begin, coming to explore
for the first time, a human being
being completely no longer out
on the cracking limb, being no
longer under the lies, being able
to apply the rights of One to themselves.

No one takes our jobs!
Stop being so unearthly white!
And begin to honour your ancestors!

Chad Norman

Till all that's left is white space

I found my body parts at the
bottom of an editor's bin
loose rinds of the lips
my mother gave me
a yanked tooth
the bridge of my brow
wilted laugh lines
shredded coils of hair
the scrunched petals of my nose
fistfuls of plump
shades of my skin
seeping out of the sides
until there was light, so much light
and I think:
this is an angelic death, isn't it?
a slow smother
an obsessive throttle
a constant murder

Selina Nwulu

98

A model scout's litany

Valentino's 'African' themed spring 2016 show featured bongo-style drumming and had models in cornrows wearing bone necklaces, feathers and safari prints. Eight out of the show's 87 looks were given to black models.

We're not hiring many black girls this season too much sass. bad attitude. jezebel. ink blot. too much chunk. ratchet. coming for you. too much *They just don't have the right aesthetic*. too much spice. thick lip. nappy knot. ink blot. baartman bounce. suffocating you. too much. *We're following what sells*. too much temptress. jungle fever bite. secret crotch creep. silent shudder. wet. too much bruise. an ink blot spoiling the clothes. too much. *We're going for a very specific look*. too much choke. rage. hip jut. grit. overspill. cheap sell. spoiling the clothes. an ink blot spoiling the clothes. too much *European. These girls tend to have fewer curves*. Keep it Simple Unsoiled Neat Keep it Straight Whip Straight Tame Flowing Keep it Clean Pure Snow Chaste Keep it Clear Flowing Mild Keep it Chic Keep it Current Keep it Perfect Keep it Now. Keep it.

Selina Nwulu

Guinea Street

Bristol's Guinea Street down by the docks
was once trodden by the feet of
Edmund Saunders and of Joseph Holbrook
Their houses hewn from local rocks
rise five tall giddy stories to the heights
propped up by twisted pillars of society
constructed from the thick congealed hot blood
cold sweat and bitter tears of slavery
No signs of beauty honour or of bravery
reside within the walls of this stern stone
for they are brittle soulless creatures
Symbols of their owners' callous greed
Money manufactured from their need
to put a price on human muscle flesh and bone

The famous guinea coin created here in Bristol
by the RAC — not the one that rescues cars —
the one that cut deep everlasting scars
upon the soul of a dismembered people
The 'Royal African Company'
Quite a respectable sounding name
but history tells us of its shame

The traders called it Guinea
That Western part of Africa
where human beings were stripped
of dignity identity and name
Torn from their homes and ancient roots
to be transported to a life of hell ...
Yet even though eventually the bell
tolled noisily ... relentlessly ...
to bring the awful business to an end
So very many generations later
weeping scars beneath the surface
yearn to mend

Sarah Nymanhall

Rage rises

Rage rises
tongues of flame
sear bones, sinew and muscle

wrapped in brown skin

limbs writhe against batons
lips swell with beatings
eyes bleed, jaw cracks

wrapped in brown skin

shackled. starved. raped.
gouged. hunted. choked.
lynched. poked. injected.

stripped. drowned. expelled.
trampled. airbrushed. kneed.
medicated. gassed. gunned

down
down
down

years of white knuckles and heels
kick up dust clouds
in cotton fields, ghettos, tower blocks

brown skin burns,
turns flesh to dust dust dust
fills nostrils, clogs windpipes

Until
I can't breathe

Revd Dr Catherine Okoronkwo

Freedom Square

Freedom is a square in Tehran
workers gather
in the early morning, waiting
to be picked up for a job.
Any job.
Sometimes building walls for a new prison
where they might end up
for struggling to have a union.

Nasrin Parvaz

Delivered Into the Arms of the New Normal

The stork cries for the June babies
that enter life's race on long sunshine
days shaded with virus, riots,
politicos lying, vying for more
than their fair share of the narrative

She flies over protesters tear-gassed
on the steps of a Washington church
as the house of prayer is hijacked,
used as a backdrop, exploited,
stage managed as a prop
by a leader who exits,
hunkers down, safely bunkered
behind his bullion as the cop shop
and courthouse burns

The stork delivers her bundle to the front
porch of a Minneapolis home. These are
the days 2020's June babies must grow
into. She flies, a tear slides down her
long red beak, hits the ground, explodes
in a slow-mo crown at the sneakered
feet of a woman born twenty Junes ago,
fist punching a hole in the sky, chanting:
Black Lives Matter

Tracey Pearson

for george

under a darkening sky
we sit round a log fire
out there cities are burning
the planet is burning and

i can't breathe

out there people are dying
in hospitals in care homes
alone in bedsits with the knee
of a cop pressed into their neck and

i can't breathe

out there pepper spray nightstick
rubber bullet rage
the same wrongs the old injustice
complicity complacency and

i can't breathe

in the darkness we search
for each other for hope
for the glimmerings of dawn
for words but what words are there
we haven't used before?

listen fucking listen

i can't breathe
i can't breathe
i can't breathe

'

steve pottinger

What I Want

I want the open sore
our country has become
to finish draining
and start healing.

I want children stolen at the border
returned to their mothers,
I want heartless bureaucrats jailed
with no parole.

I want kneeling
football players
awarded trophies
for honoring the fallen.

I want the ancestors
to gather, sing us songs
of solidarity
stroke our brows while we sleep.

I want to see the homeless rise
from subway grates, park benches
I want their empty bowls filled
with opportunity and blessing

Just once,
I want to see billionaires
breaking bread with former felons,
single moms, runaways, bag ladies.

I want the mothers and grandmothers
to have enough time, enough money,
enough food to feed and nurture
all who come to the table.

I want to see reconciliation
trump racism. I want to see law
infused with love. I want
compassion as our currency.

The time has come
balance the books,
clean the rivers,
heal our history.

Judith Prest

Cotton Thread

Here you are, sauntering from the park,
waving goodbye to your friend at the corner,
checking your tight, black curls in the newsagent's window;
back to my cottage where you show me a loose cotton thread
on your High School Musical T-shirt. You pull it.
No! I say, *It'll fall apart.*
You giggle, share the thread with me – *Pull it, Nan.*
And I do. And we laugh as a whole seam unravels.

You and I holding a thread so easily broken –
there you are, wearing a crimson headscarf, carrying
a big blue bowl of mangoes on your head, strong
legs rolling beneath you, arms pushing you on
down a white dusty road, brown eyes fixed
on another grandmother's home.

Marilyn Ricci

Awaken

In a bombed-out street, wind moves the lips
of a politician on a poster. Ilya Kaminsky

This is not a bombed-out country
but the hospitals are suddenly
full of dying black women who
do not know a word of English.
They are older than Snowdonia, the
Pennines, Ben Lomond, Ben Nevis. Yet
they are as young as you or I.
The doctors can't seem to diagnose
any sickness, yet their vitals are
fading fast. The papers are full
of the news, thousands of black
women who know that truth
is dying. They have given birth
to generations of Africans, Australians,
Americans, they know where blood
comes from. They don't know what
a mobile phone is or any kind of computer,
yet they're all connected, every one of them
loses another breath, another heartbeat,
at the exact same hour, across the land.
They breathe as one together. They die
as one together. The doctors don't know
what to do. The papers are full of the news,
thousands of black women who know the truth
and don't speak our native tongue, are dying.
Deep within, we know their ancient wisdom,
but we've forgotten it. Our only hope
is to dream their dying breath into us,
breathe their truth into our dreams,
awake with their language on our lips.

Bethany Rivers

Suffrage

The lilac crocus
against the green
stirs spring to life.

Lilac and green
reflects a vision
of hope and strength;

still to come
for those still born
in barren climes,

and sisters shot
or buried to face
not warming sun,

but stone so sharp
it kills life
before it has formed.

No. Seed is strong
it springs to life
not purple and green,

just slashed with warmth
a summer fruit
Malala scented.

Jenny Robb

Your Name

Shukri Yahye-Abdi, I'm so sorry.

I do not know how you came to this land,
the one called En-ger-land, with an ugly
jeer in its heart. I do know that you came
by way of Kenya from Somalia,
and grew up in a refugee camp.
I think of rows of tents or shacks, not much
else in a barren tract. And then a journey
to a rainy town of edifices,
a ruined abbey, a monument to Peel,
schools, a countryside park with deep mill ponds,
and the much-vaunted open-air market.
When you settled there in Bury
did you think, at last, a place I can breathe
and branch out in, reaching for the normal
possibilities? In the photograph
the newspapers published of you
your eyes are curious and radiant
and your twelve-year-old self is beautiful
as a stream joining a wider river.
When they forced you into the Irwell, what
kind of baptism did they envisage?
What return of ancient witch trials, this?
Well, what they have buried in the water
is their own youth, their childhoods ever now
silted with that night, and I am so saddened,
Shukri Yahye-Abdi, that the English
failed to make this green land a place
where to receive your gift of gentleness.

Caroline Rooney

Icarus

Cain was there
when they hid
the murder of Icarus.
And where did they get
those old school photos
that make him
look criminal, still?

Crowd-a-come
to watch them raise Icarus
without statue binds.
Yet he isn't Lazarus.
So instead let them gather
in Bristol around Colston
and take wonky
underwater photos of him.
Our history skewed.

Let Icarus become
an accidental martyr.
We'll celebrate lockdown parole
queuing at Primark.
But George Floyd
could have been you.

And when done with
those hashtagged meme slogans
the dailies reference in
their half-page obituaries,
let's all half-clap on
half-beat to match
the rhythm of their
indifference

At the bus stop. Overheard.
The same tired and bitter half-credits
and here's a few:
1. All Lives Matter
2. These things will happen.
3. Everyone calm down.

4. It happened so far away.

And how do I know Icarus?

Icarus had a sister.
She fell for me.
I fell for her too.
I took her to Dalston.
We sat in a blues.
We fell from the speaker.
We fell from the sound.
And when the party was over
we fell to the ground

Eddie Saint-Jean

Coda

Land is not my school, my history,
my land was never disembowelled for gain,

nor have I roots grown down so deep in it
that in my bones I know it to be mine.

I am not subject to The Season's laws,
nor do they govern where I stay or go.

I have no Homeland to be taken back,
no drum to beat that no one listens to,

no shaman to recover what I've lost,
no Frog to heal or teach me to be wise,

no Elders to pass on the lore, learned
from the throat songs of my ancestors.

Language was not stolen from my mouth,
nor did my children grow up separate.

I cannot know how loss makes warriors
or hold a potlatch for your ancient grief,

but fashion stories with a poets tongue,
your stories walking in my skin,

make them anew and give them back,
of rights, of heritage, your living land.

Chrys Salt

From the mid 19th century to the mid 90s the Canadian Government separated thousands of Inuit children from their parents and placed them in schools run by the church ostensibly to 'assimilate' them. They were taught their belief systems were wrong, were forbidden to speak their language or exercise their culture.

What the lookout saw
(Beaver Mountain 1897)

The Yukon winds its arms
round inlets, reed beds, stranded isles,
glacial silt washed down from mountains
to the river's lip,
sheer sand banks undercut by currents,
pocked with swallows' nests

He's standing where he always stands,
high on the warty outcrop,
look-out for bark canoes,
graceful and marvellously light,
skimming towards his village with their wares -

but not for this, this
silence shredded to a din,
these shrieking clouds,
this spume, this smash,
this loud flotilla on the water snake.
How could there be so many in the world?

Swift on his moccasins
he scrambles down.
He shouts in the fields,
he shouts in the fish camp.
He runs like the hare to tell them,
tells them the white man comes again,
lights fires on their land,
takes fish for dog food,
scares the moose
cuts down trees,
tramples the sweet-grass
makes rivers run backwards,
turns mountains inside out.

'Until our fallen warriors return,
the wise Chief says,
'we will be moose calves in a land of wolves'

Chrys Salt

Skating at Black Lives Matter Plaza

For Kaitlyn Saunders

black/ lives/ matter/ most
when they are in motion
Patricia Smith: Incendiary Art, Ferguson 2014

In yellow and white leotard, Kaitlyn Saunders
tilts into the yellow B of
BLACK
LIVES
MATTER

Rise Up sings Andra Day. The family rises early.
Early morning at the plaza, the streets are empty.
She holds in her head routines, jumps and spins.

She is nine years old.
This moment of happiness matters.

She skates, skimming over double yellow lines,
recently pristine letters
slightly worn, muddy

like a home of marchers   skate-boarders
weaving   light-footed   light-headed
with   momentum   of history

She wants to share her hopes
this feeling of being free she gets skating,
she wishes everyone could be free.

I felt like I was floating and it was limitless
she says, as if she were a whirling dervish
spinning into something infinitely bigger.

A black girl in yellow and white leotard
tilting into the yellow B of
BLACK
LIVES
MATTER
at the plaza

home of marchers   skate-boarders
weaving   light-footed   light-headed
with   momentum   of history

Barbara Saunders

Statues for Black Lives Matter
For Clive Myrie

When those roots aren't there, when the branches of the family tree are
broken, there's a sadness and a sense you're almost floating through life,
untethered to the ground.
Clive Myrie: Racism and statues: How the toxic legacy of empire still
affects us. BBC website 7th July 2020

All this is true, you look to
painted records of your life
There are no other records

And you see a statue
The family you leave behind
disappear in a crack of history
...   .

Slow broken English hides
languages they laugh in
rocking body and soul

This song of longing
a lullaby they have sung
...   .

This song of longing
I hear you singing
a baby asleep in your grand-

mother's mother's mother's
mother's mother's mother's
mother's mother's arms

All this is true
He knew what he was doing
His statue shows no remorse

Barbara Saunders

Bad Sail

Another tyrant cast in bronze
is cast into the harbour,
while far-off in Atlantic's bed
still lie the twenty-thousand
branded by his iron — jettisoned
for the crime of being dead.

Its wake is wide,
this Royal African Company ship
which forges on
against the good will of the tide.
Its bad sail is our silence — blocking out
the wisdom of the sun.

Joel Scarfe

Rashan Charles

Dalston, Hackney.
Bins and street furniture, set on fire.
Pictures of a young man on a poster in the flames,
The words: *"This could be you next."*

Beamed live on the news, through the night.
At home I watch... my leg in plaster...
I know Kingsland Road... but...
That secure feeling that this pain is not mine.

They repeat his name.
I freeze.
Not Rashan.
My son's school, me on playground duty.

Not Rashan... the boy you wanted to wrap up from the cold.
Not Rashan... who stoically accepted the good life was not for him.

Yes Rashan on the CCTV footage
held down on the floor, suffocating...
Posted to YouTube.
And we watched him die.

The police claimed Rashan was "taken ill"
and an officer intervened to help him.
Not True.

Yes we are angry.

The boy wincing in the sun, third from the back.
School photo.
Struggling with so much.
Child Protection Register.
In my class, Year 3.
Shopping for the eldery, nursing small kittens.
Yes Rashan.
Struggling to breathe.
A member of the public entitled to sit on him.
The policeman with his fingers in Rashan's mouth.

"Resisting Arrest"?
You know Rashan -
You know he processes information differently?

Be careful of the media.
Because Rashan was gentle. Innit?

Rashan was also 20 years old.
He could have been your friend.

Rashan Charles
Died 22nd July 2017
corner of Middleton Road.

Lily Silverman

The Black Death

Snide barbs prick to see what colour you bleed,
but for now you have given up bleeding.
Your blood has congealed cold, black and clotted,
infected by the old contagion,- hate.

Vitriol seeps out accidentally.
This Black Death is a sneak thief taking lives.
Its weapons are selective and precise.

Four hundred years of genocide repeats
And they are still trying to wipe you out?

Stories run deep under time's thick layers
His story is history, it repeats.

You can't seem to stop the trajectory.
Somebody somewhere is fighting for breath.

Another victim of the old Black Death.

Suzan Spence

Statue of a South African Woman and Child

by sculptor Anne Davidson, commissioned by the city of Edinburgh District Council to honour all those killed or imprisoned in South Africa for their stand against apartheid, unveiled in 1986.

What does she see, this woman
from a township far away, placed here
with her child in Scotland's capital,
fixed at street level, no pedestal,
smeared with lipstick by some joker,
making her eyes appear to bleed?
Is that what she sees – blood –
the flood of it, from Sharpeville and Nyanga,
washing in waves out to the Atlantic,
all the way to the North Sea and into Leith,
its crimson tinge lapping at *Britannia's* hull,
the floating palace, global ambassador, that sailed
with fanfare one sunlit morning into Table Bay,
taking our Queen to shake Mandela's hand,
her crown jewels' Cape diamonds mined
in the currency of blood?

Gerda Stevenson

Rejected

hospital smock
replacing suit
he's tube threaded
by a window
too high for trees

his whisky smuggled
in shampoo bottles
tupperware curries
with hot buttered naan
ordered in Urdu

we pilgrim here
bring you *The Jang*
remember - once
you signed treaties
you brokered deals

but now you're just
a wilting plant
placed in the sun
waiting for water
needing tending now

but not anyone
not by their hands, no
and you say a word
I've been shielded from
'habshi'- a slave and

we crumble down
shamed and fuming
chase after heels
scramble sorries
that don't add up

to the cuts he's caused
we know their sting too
but haven't suffered
this - its rusted barb
and watch him refuse

all Black care
as proper doctors
and all good nurses
are White preferably
or Asian sometimes

Laila Sumpton

The Jang is a Pakistani newspaper.

And don't call me a 'person of colour'.

Samir Sweida-Metwally

Popo

I used to be so fond of Popo
when I was a child
I wished to, longed to, be just like Him
badge and gun, in blue
He was so smart
He was so strong
He shot the baddies,
never wrong
I knew that Popo cared for me
and worked to keep me safe
He only beat me, bruised my face
to teach me lessons, mnemonically
but as I grew I noticed that my
Popo seemed to change
His will grew weaker, temper short
composure lost for rage
He'd stop and search for profiled souls
but not for answers, not
his own
He now seemed scared and vulnerable
to shadows real or not,
to pressures from the suited smilers
pushing targets, jail the rot
Aims now wavered, purpose faltered
stabbed into the dark-
-er skinned and poorer neighbours,
knee upon a dream
I see encrusted, dry saliva
splats from when His skills,
applied forensically to skulls –
red scabs on thin blue lies
Still we love Him, need Him here
to serve, surveil, subdue
despite the change
that never was –
in Who he saves, from us

George Symonds

Whitman, Lennon, 'Saints and 'Scroungers'

The Council's posting posters: 'Proud of Notts',
above the city, high rise skeletons host calling workmen.
Broadmarsh, seventies eyesore, now just craters
and, local news, two bailiffs find a man at home -
starved to death.

You can't make poems from this, just be recording angel.

Walt Whitman had it right, someone, divine as anyone,
is dead (a scrounging government office clawing-
back his means) official letters don't apologise.

Just be recording angel, you can't make poems from this.

Still, on the wall they're: 'proud of Notts, ambitious' for their city
'and its people', a man, divine as you, or me, is dead.
Perhaps Lennon's shade could lyricise cold-
water flats, or public faces left in jars by doors?
Though even he might struggle.

A man (last weight under five stone) is dead,
let ghost Whitman or Lennon make a poem from this,
let them stand, supreme recording angels,
defacing posters boasting 'Proud of Notts':
with 'funeral blues', for all the lonely people.

Deborah Tyler-Bennett

On Errol Graham (aged 57), from Nottingham, starved to death after his benefits
were stopped/ Funeral blues – reference to W.H. Auden poem title.

Shame

I betrayed you
Like Judas I denied you
and so I live with shame

My childhood friend
I watched you from the window
As you stepped on the bus

I made to catch your eye
As you made your way along
Eager to reminisce

But a crowd of youths
Brave in their pack
Baited and berated you

You handled yourself
With dignity
As they spewed their venom

An object of hate
for the colour of your skin
and for being a woman

Whilst I hid in my seat
Now trying to remain
Invisible to your eyes

Scared I would become
The target of hate
Through association

Cheryl Vallely

My Dungeon Shook Again

London

A young black father comes to the parents' meeting.
The white headteacher makes him angry
with talk of new expectations and raising the bar.
Expectations are not the problem.
What makes you think your school will succeed,
you'll have too many black kids?
His question brings gasps from black mothers
who turn to reprimand him.
I'd go private if I could afford it.
They've heard his words but not the fear
of what will happen to his son, at this time,
in this city, on this sceptr'd isle.

A Mother's Love and Fear

A black mother holds the headteacher's hand,
she has an eleven-year-old son,
her grip tightens, her eyes plead –
Keep my son alive, sir.

Chicago

In a school assembly hall on the South Side of Chicago
young black men do not compromise,
they recite their creed – every one of us is college-bound.
The black colleague from London looks to the heavens,
says to himself on a cold Thursday in February, this is where I
        belong.
A block away four young black men are gunned down in broad
        daylight.

PR Walker

The title is a reference to James Baldwin's famous letter to his nephew in "The
Fire Next Time".

129

You do not go to the riot

You do not go   to the riot
the riot comes   to you
it crashes   through your brain
hacks   into your blood stream
breaks   your
bones
black eyes   weeping
black blood   bleeding
a transmission a transfusion a translation
a nation of
pink cheeks green faces
helmuts and fever
the redmeat   President
holds
a cleaver
orders   children   with dark skin
arrested
at the school gate
criminals smack
their heads
tell them
they will NOT breathe they are
dead
pink cheeks and green faces
no one
is the right   colour
only the blood is
the same

Patricia Welles

This rage
A response to Trevor Noah's words: "Police in America are looting Black lives"

this rage
roars like a brushfire
new blazes sparking every minute
this rage
is oxygen-starved despair
predating its current triggers
this rage
is unheeded histories
consuming all in their path
this rage
is pure and full of grief
for all the looted lives
this rage
demands we hear and see and feel –
this rage
demands justice at last

Michele Witthaus

Phantoms

Guns and chains went in,
rubber and ivory came out.
Sorrows and tusks and ruthless greed
imported through Antwerp's frenzied port.

Cruel inhumanity within, the tattered string,
grey rotting cord, yesterday's phantoms in a row.
History stains this old family heirloom.
Time for the Phantom-King to climb down.

When the old local jeweller attempts
his restringing, will these beads be truly cleansed?
Or, do the phantoms permeate too far and too deep,
too far and too evil to tolerate?

Frothing cataracts at Kisangani,
the severed rigid hands, the rows of heads.
The tent of fear, ten million dead.
What did ten million Black Lives matter?

Timidly in tattered shadowy old photos,
she navigates her way back down the aisle
on the taut elbow of her proud groom,
ensnared in a horror-rope of ivory beads.

Leopold's statues adorned the streets,
school history texts all lied, how would
a naïve young Antwerp bride begin to know
of cruelty, exploitation, and hypocrisy.

Guns and chains went in,
rubber and ivory came out,
a society grew rich and ignored
the long tentacles of complicity.

Phantoms persist in these haughty statues.
Each and every Leopold - the original criminal
of the phrase "crime against humanity" –
must go!

Kathy Zwick

"This choice of nightmares (was) forced upon me in the tenebrous land invaded by the mean and greedy phantoms," Marlow in Joseph Conrad's *Heart of Darkness*, 1902

"Taking down statues is important on the symbolic level, but it is just the beginning. These monuments are present not just in public space, but also in people's mentalities," Ms Joelle Sambi Nzeba, spokeswoman for Belgian Network for Black Lives, June 2020

Contributors

Peter A's work has been published online and in paper publications including *Laldy, Spindrift, Poems for Grenfell Tower, A Kist of Thistles,* both Dove Tales anthologies *A Kind of Stupidity* and *Bridges or Walls?, Surfing* and *Angry Manifesto.* His first chapbook *Art of Insomnia* will be launched in late 2020/early 2021.

'Funmi Adewole is a dance academic, writer and performer with an interest in the arts and cultural citizenship.

Mayo Agard-Olubo is a web designer, writer and poet based in London. You can find more of his poetry at https://medium.com/@MayoPoetry

Sandra A. Agard is a professional storyteller, writer, cultural historian and literary consultant. She was born in Hackney, London to Guyanese parents, and is the author of *Harriet Tubman: A Journey to Freedom* (Stripes Publishing Ltd, an imprint of the Little Tiger Group, UK and USA, 2019). Her short stories have been published in *Tales, Myths and Legends* (Scholastic, 1991), *Time for Telling* (Kingfisher, 1991) and *Unheard Voices* (Corgi Books, an imprint of Random House Children's Books, 2007).

Jim Aitken is a poet and dramatist who also works with people with mental health issues. He has edited *A Kist of Thistles* (2020) - a radical collection of Scottish Poetry published by Culture Matters and has read his work at Love Music, Hate Racism events in Scotland.

Nick Allen has published one collection ("the riding") and two pamphlets of poetry. He helps organise *Rhubarb at the Triangle*, a spoken word evening in Shipley. He is an active Trade Unionist in West Yorkshire where he talks with poets in the back rooms of pubs and sometimes feels enlightened.

Rosalie Alston wanted to go on the Black Lives Matter march in Bristol on June 7th 2020 but was held back by being over sixty during Coronavirus Lockdown. She witnessed the statue of slave-trader Colston eerily hanging upside-down outside a museum, after retrieval from Bristol Harbour, where protesters had dumped it.

Judith Amanthis, a Londoner, has published short fiction in UK literary magazines including Dead Ink, Tears in the Fence, and Over the Red Line, and her journalism has been published in Ghana, South Africa and the UK. Her novel *Dirt Clean* was published by Victorina Press in November 2019.

Adrienne Asher lives in Sunrise Florida USA with her husband Steven. She works as a paraprofessional at an elementary school. She is 55 and has been writing poetry since the age of 12.

Mellow Baku has performed spoken word and music at New York Knitting Factory, London Southbank, Curve Theatre. Associate Artist with The Spark Arts for Children, *Yellow Book* panel assessor for Rethink Your Mind (2015-19), Leicester Jazz House Board Director, co-curator of poetry and music event Moonshine Word Jam, she facilitates for NHS produced BrightSparks & Word!

Sharon Cherry Ballard has worked extensively on screen and stage as an actress, singer and more recently as a writer/producer. As an actress, she has worked on some of the UK's most popular TV shows including BBC's Sherlock and Eastenders. As a black creative, Sharon is dedicated to writing and producing innovative work that highlight the importance of representation.

Panya Banjoko is a UK based poet, playwright and PhD candidate at Nottingham Trent University. Her debut collection of poetry, *Some Things*, was published by Burning Eye Books (2018). Panya is a multi-award-winning poet, co-ordinates a Black Writers Network, and is patron for Nottingham UNESCO City of Literature.

Tanisha Barrett is a mental health nurse, delivering therapy and also teaching about diversity and difference. She is a proud, black queer woman who is very passionate about dismantling systemic inequalities. In her spare time, she writes poems about mental health, race, sexuality and body image. www.blacksugarising.com Instagram @blacksugarising

Originally from Aberdeen, **Lesley Benzie** has lived in Glasgow for 25+ years, working and raising her family. There her vernacular was novelty and impetus for writing, resulting in magazines/anthology publication and her first collection, SEWN UP. 2020 saw her second collection, FESSEN, a 'Highly Commended' in the Vernal Equinox and 'Runner up' in the Mc-Cash Scots Poetry Competitions.

Conor Blessing is a self-taught writer with work normally published to exhibitions held by CultureNL. He can be found at the Creative Writing Class of the Bellshill Cultural Centre.

Tim Bombdog is Leicester's very own post-punk anarchic poet combining hard hitting revolutionary poetry with wit, humour and a touch of sensitivity. He is a people's poet whose work is rooted in a certain time and place, but is compassionate, challenging, unique and of interest to all.

Some of **Richard Byrt**'s work, as a published poet, and for two LGBT+ history projects, explores reasons, individually and in society, for offensive, discriminatory beliefs and actions. Writing about these topics is not intended to cause hurt and offence (apologies if it does), but, hopefully, increases his self-reflection and understanding.

Julian Colton has had five collections of poetry published including *Everyman Street* (Smokestack Publishing), *Cold Light of Morning* (Cultured Llama) and *Two Che Guevaras* (Scottish Borders Council). He edits *The Eildon Tree* literary magazine and contributes articles and reviews. He lives in Selkirk in the Scottish Borders.

Mark Connors is a poet and novelist from Leeds. His poetry pamphlet, *Life is a Long Song* was published by OWF Press in 2015. His first collection, *Nothing is Meant to be Broken* was published by Stairwell Books in 2017. His second collection, *Optics*, was published by YAFFLE in 2019. www.markconnors.co.uk

John Cooper writes short fiction and verse as much for pleasure as anything else. He now lives and works in Hampshire, having been born and lived most of his life in Suffolk.

Tracy Davidson lives in Warwickshire, England, and writes poetry and flash fiction. Her work has appeared in various publications and anthologies, including: Poet's Market, Mslexia, Atlas Poetica, Modern Haiku, The Binnacle, A Hundred Gourds, Shooter, Journey to Crone, The Great Gatsby Anthology, WAR, In Protest: 150 Poems for Human Rights.

Giles Dawnay is a trainee GP and writer based in Herefordshire. Prior to becoming a Doctor he travelled extensively in Latin America, West Africa and the South Pacific, seeing all too well the marginalization of peoples through things as arbitrary as colour and appearance.

Martins Deep (he/him) is a Nigerian student, poet, photographer, & boy child advocate. He is passionate about documenting muffled stories of the African experience in his poetry & visual art. His works have appeared on Barren Magazine, Variant Literature, Mineral Lit Mag, Agbowó Magazine & elsewhere.

Sara Eliot is a published poet and singer/songwriter. She has performed in London, Paris and L.A. She currently plays gigs around London. She also works as Poetry Tutor for an arts organisation.

Blake Everitt (b. 1989) lives on the Isle of Wight and has had poems published in *Plumwood Mountain: An Australian Journal of Ecopoetry and Ecopoetics*, *Harbinger Asylum* (Texas), *Pensive: A Global Journal of Spirituality and the Arts* (MA), *Time of Singing* (Pennsylvania), *The Poetry Village*, *Black Lives Matter UK*, *Quarr Abbey Newsletter*, *Littoral Magazine*, *Eye Flash Poetry*, *The Recusant*, *Dead Beats*, *Friendly Fire Collective* (Philadelphia), *C.H.S newsletter,* the anthology *Book of Christian Poems*, and *The Blue Morphosis* by GreenFingers Recordings. He has poems forthcoming in *Hawk & Whippoorwill* (MA), and T*he Dawntreader*.

Ravelle-Sadé Fairman is a self-proclaimed accidental poet and mental health advocate. After realising the impact of her honesty, she has been actively overcoming her own issues to share her insight with others through her "Poetic Perception". Ravelle-Sadé is passionate about trying to address society's taboos in the hope that it may help others to see that they aren't alone.

Mike Farren has been 'canto' winner for Poem of the North and placed / shortlisted / commended in several other competitions. His pamphlets are 'Pierrot and his Mother' (Templar) and 'All of the Moons' (Yaffle). He is part of the Yaffle publishing team and co-hosts Rhubarb Open Mic in Shipley.

Paul Francis is a retired teacher living in Much Wenlock, Shropshire. He is active as a writer and performer in the West Midlands poetry scene, and is also the author of several pamphlets as well as *Sonnets with notes* (2019). During lockdown he posted a sonnet a day, at www.paulfranciswrites.co.uk/paulfrancispoems?category=Sonnets

Michelle Fuller lives in the UK and formerly worked in the NHS for nine years. Having experienced the UK immigration 'hostile environment', she uses her creative works to raise awareness of the system's injustices. "Tales of a Hostile Kingdom", an animation based on her writing, depicting the hostile environment was produced by Refugee Journalism Project www.refugeejournalismproject.org/2019/11/01/tales-of-a-hostile-kingdom-2/

Harry Gallagher's poetry has been published by Orbis, IRON, Smokestack, The Interpreter's House, Prole and many others. His books include *Northern Lights* (Stairwell Books, 2017) and *Running Parallel* (Black Light Engine Room, 2019). He runs the Tyne & Wear stanza of the Poetry Society. www.harrygallagherpoet.wordpress.com

Mike Gallagher, an award winning Irish poet, editor and facilitator, has been published throughout the world and translated into several languages. His collection, *Stick on Stone*, is published by Revival Press.

Moira Garland lives in Leeds. Her poetry appears in magazines including *The North*, and in anthologies such as *And The Stones Fell Open*. Her poem won the 2016 Leeds Peace Poetry Competition. A retired melodeon player, and ex-college lecturer she can be found here: @moiragauthor and occasionally: www.wordswords-moirag.blogspot.com

Kathy Gee's career was in heritage. Her poetry collection, *Book of Bones* was published by V. Press in 2016 and she wrote the spoken word elements for *Suite For The Fallen Soldier*, a narrative suite of choral music commemorating World War I, which premiered on Armistice Day 2016. Her small collection of duologues, *Checkout*, set in a corner shop, was published in March 2019. www.brainginger.co.uk

Rachel Glass has had several poems published in anthologies by Valley Press and Riza Press. Other poems have been included in online publications such as Polemical and Wild Roof Journal. She can usually be found writing, drinking hot chocolate and wearing glittery shoes.

Lind Grant-Oyeye is a poet of African descent. She is the recipient of multiple poetry awards including the Ken Saro-Wiwa poetry award. She believes art can be used as a voice for reforms and healing.

Prabhu S. Guptara's poems have been published since the 1960s in magazines, in anthologies, and in two collections. In January 2017, Skylark Publications, UK, chose him as its Poet of the Month. He is included in Debrett's *People of Today*.

Nusrat M Haider has been working in housing, health and social care for more than 15 years. She likes reading novels, poetry, history and sci fi.

Jean Hall is a Brit Born London based writer of African and Caribbean heritage. Her writing has appeared in *Power Writers and the Struggle Against Slavery* (Pub. Hansib 2005) and *Red: an Anthology of Contemporary Black British Poetry* (Pub. Peepal Tree 2010).

Whilst working with a charity to support family carers, **Roger Hare** rediscovered a love for poetry. Since retiring he is enjoying further experiments with words and how they can bring to life his observations of the world. He's grateful that poems have found a home in various places in print and online. He can be found on Twitter @RogerHare6

Samantha Harper-Robins has previously been aired on BBC Wiltshire Radio and BBCUpload Festival 2020. @SamanthaDance7

Deborah Harvey's poems have been widely published in journals and anthologies, broadcast on Radio 4's Poetry Please, and awarded several major prizes. Her fifth poetry collection, *Learning Finity*, will be published by Indigo Dreams in 2021. She is co-director of The Leaping Word poetry consultancy.

Jem Henderson has an MA in Creative Writing from York St. John University. She has been published in Kanstellation, The Writers' Cafe Magazine, Wyrd Words and Effigies, Beautiful Scruffiness, Down in the Dirt, and various publications online. She is working on her first collection and novel.

Kevin Higgins's *Song of Songs 2.0: New & Selected Poems* was published in 2017 by Salmon. The Stinging Fly magazine has described Kevin as "likely the most read living poet in Ireland. His poems have been quoted in *The Daily Telegraph, The Times* (UK), *The Independent, The Daily Mirror, Hot Press* magazine, and read aloud by film director Ken Loach at a political meeting in London. Kevin's eighth poetry collection, *Sex and Death at Merlin Park Hospital*, was published by Salmon Poetry in June 2019 and one of the poems from it will feature in the next, and final, novel in Ken Bruen's Jack Taylor series.

Arun Jeetoo is a wanderer who possesses the gift of compassion known for his dirty realism style of work, provocative and raw imagery and dark humour, he asks his readers to reflect on what it means to be human in the 21st century. Check out his poetry on Instagram @G2poetry.

Hamdi Khalif is a writer born in Mogadishu, the capital of Somalia and raised in London. Between 2015 and 2016, she toured with her poetry collective Bards without Borders on their show, "Shakespeare is dead get over it!", and in 2019, she completed an MA in Creative Writing.

Kihwa-Endale is an artist based in Helsinki. She uses spoken word and poetry to express the things that cannot be translated visually.

Tom Krause is a 25-time contributing author to the *Chicken Soup for the Soul* book series, a teacher/coach in Missouri Public Schools for 31 years (retired) and, over the past 20 years, a national motivational speaker.

Laurie Kuntz is an award-winning poet and film producer. She published one poetry collection (*Somewhere in the Telling*, Mellen Press), two chapbooks (*Simple Gestures,* Texas Review Press and *Women at the Onsen,* Blue Light Press). Her new poetry collection, *The Moon Over My Mother's House* is forthcoming from Finishing Line Press in 2021. Recently retired, she lives in an endless summer state of mind. Visit her at https://lauriekuntz.myportfolio.com/home-1

D.L. Lang is the author of 13 poetry books, most recently *This Festival of Dreams*. She served as poet laureate of Vallejo, California from 2017 to 2019. Her poems have been transformed into songs, Jewish liturgy, and used to advocate for peace and justice. Her website is poetryebook.com

Charles G Lauder, Jr, was born and raised in Texas and has lived in the UK since 2000. His poems have appeared internationally and his debut collection, *The Aesthetics of Breath*, was published in 2019 by V.Press.

Born in Lima, Peru, immigrating to Los Angeles at age 4, **Adriano Timoteo Llosa** holds a BA in Political Science, field organized for Barack Obama in 2008, and worked in the US Labor Department. An existential crisis became the journey into spirituality and performing arts. He plans to explore Asia and Africa.

Rob Lowe writes and publishes accessible verse. He is currently reading The Auschwitz Poems. He believes poetry can change societies for the better. His most recent work is in Dwell Time 2, and in an RSPB anthology, with work pending in Seventh Quarry and The Green Light.

Paul Lyalls is a one time poet for the Roald Dahl Family and Museum and has worked on the London 2012 Olympics and gigged with Lemn Sissay, Kate Tempest and even Rasta Mouse! He gives amazing performances and workshops in schools. www.paul-lyalls.uk

Margaret Mair, blessed – or cursed – with an adventurous bent, explores words, ideas, experiences and places. Born in Jamaica into a multi-hued family, she long ago chose to be a citizen of Canada where she lives on her boat on a lake as far south as possible.

Isabella Mead is Head of Learning at The Story Museum in Oxford. She won the Wells Poetry Competition 2019, judged by Simon Armitage. Her poetry frequently appears in Poetry News. She has been Highly Commended twice in the Bridport Prize (2016 and 2019), and longlisted in the National Poetry Competition (2017).

Lester Gómez Medina is a Nicaraguan-Costa Rican writer of poetry and narrative. He studied Spanish Philology at the UCR in San José, Costa Rica. Since 2014, he has lived in London where he completed an MA on Audio-visual Translation at the University of Roehampton (2018).

Maureen Mguni is a Technical Instructor and Doctoral Researcher at the School of Applied Social Science, University of Brighton. She is also a registered senior social worker and a Female Genital Mutilation/Cutting (FGM/C) Consultant. She campaigns against human rights abuse; systemic racism; Violence against Women and Girls (VAWG) and child poverty.

Jenny Mitchell is winner of the Aryamati Poetry Prize; the Segora Poetry Prize; a Bread and Roses Poetry Award; the Fosseway Poetry Prize; joint winner of the Geoff Stevens Memorial Prize; and a 2 x Best of the Net Nominee. A debut collection, *Her Lost Language*, is one of 44 Poetry Books for 2019 (Poetry Wales) and a Jhalak Prize #bookwelove Recommendation. Twitter: @jennymitchellgo

Leanne Moden is a poet, performer and theatre-maker from Nottingham. She has performed at events across the UK and Europe, including WOMAD Festival, the Edinburgh Fringe, Sofar Sounds, and Bestival on the Isle of Wight. Her latest pamphlet was published by Burning Eye Books in July 2020. www.leannemoden.com

Cheryl Moskowitz is a US born poet, novelist and playwright. Previous publications include novel *Wyoming Trail* (Granta), *The Girl is Smiling* (Circle Time Press), poetry for children *Can it Be About Me?* (Frances Lincoln). Forthcoming publications in Spring 2021: pamphlet *Maternal Impressions* (Against the Grain Press) and *The Corona Collection* poetry exploring children's experience of the pandemic (Troika Books).

Hubert Moore's latest collection is *The Feeding Station* (Shoestring, 2019). Much of his work is informed by experience as a writing-mentor at Freedom from Torture and as a detainee-visitor. Recently he has been involved as a supporter of *Refugee Tales* in their campaign against unlimited Immigration Detention.

Loraine Masiya Mponela is a social justice campaigner living in England. Loraine has a lovely son.

Ambrose Musiyiwa coordinates Journeys in Translation, an international, volunteer-driven project that is translating poems from *Over Land, Over Sea: Poems for those seeking refuge* (Five Leaves Publications, 2015) into other languages. He edited books that include *Bollocks to Brexit: an Anthology of Poems and Short Fiction* (CivicLeicester, 2019) and *Leicester 2084 AD: New Poems about The City* (CivicLeicester, 2018). He is the author of *The Gospel According to Bobba*.

Linda Nabasa is a performing artist in Kampala Uganda. A poet, playwright, actress and theatre producer. In 2015 she co-founded Afroman Spice, a women's theatre company and in 2017 she started Blac Anthem, a theatre collaborative. She currently writes the "Luuka and Ttesa" children's rights book series.

Russell Nichols is a speculative fiction writer and endangered journalist. Raised in Richmond, California, he now lives out of a backpack with his wife, vagabonding around the world since 2011. His work revolves around concepts of race, mental health, technology, and the absurdity of existence. Look for him at www.russellnichols.com.

Chad Norman lives beside the high-tides of the Bay of Fundy, Truro, Nova Scotia. He has given talks and readings in Denmark, Sweden, Wales, Ireland, Scotland, America, and across Canada. His poems appear in publications around the world and have been translated into Danish, Albanian, Romanian, Turkish, Italian, and Polish. His collections are *Selected & New Poems* (Mosaic Press), and *Squall: Poems In The Voice Of Mary Shelley* (Guernica Editions).

Selina Nwulu is an independent consultant and writer with a commitment to social and climate justice. She has written for a number of outlets such as the Guardian, New Humanist and Red Pepper and has toured her poetry extensively, both internationally and throughout the UK. She was Young Poet Laureate for London 2015-6 and her first collection, *The Secrets I Let Slip* is a Poetry Book Society recommendation.

Sarah Nymanhall lives and writes in Bristol UK. She often creates poems with performance in mind, in the belief that live presentation of poetry lifts it from the page and can impact upon an audience in profound, and challenging ways.

Revd Dr Catherine Okoronkwo is an Anglican priest and serves as a Vicar in Swindon. Her first collection of poetry, *Blood and Water*, will be published in the autumn by Waterloo Press.

Nasrin Parvaz became a civil rights activist when the Islamic regime took power in 1979. She was arrested in 1982, and spent eight years in prison. Her books are, *One Woman's Struggle in Iran, A Prison Memoir*, and *The Secret Letters from X to A* (Victorina Press 2018). http://nasrinparvaz.org/

Tracey Pearson lives in the North East of England. She is a poet and short story writer.

Alexandros Plasatis is an ethnographer who writes fiction in English, his second language. His work has appeared in magazines and anthologies in the UK, US, India and Canada. His first book, *Made by Sea and Wood, in Darkness: a Novel in Stories*, is forthcoming from Spuyten Duyvil.

Steve Pottinger is an engaging and accomplished performer who has performed at Ledbury and StAnza poetry festivals, at the Edinburgh Free Fringe, and in venues the length and breadth of the country. His sixth volume of poems, *thirty-one small acts of love and resistance* published by Ignite Books, is out now.

Judith Prest is a poet, photographer, mixed media artist and creativity coach. Her chapbook *After* was published in 2019 by Finishing Line Press and her poems appear in anthologies and literary journals. Judith has given writing and art workshops at retreat centers, schools, prisons, retirement communities and writing conferences. Judith lives in Duanesburg, NY, USA.

Marilyn Ricci is a poet, playwright and editor. Her poetry has appeared in many small press magazines including *Magma*, *The Rialto* and *Modern Poetry in Translation*. Her pamphlet, *Rebuilding a Number 39*, was published by HappenStance Press and her first full collection, *Night Rider*, is available from SoundsWrite Press.

Bethany Rivers has two collections: *the sea refuses no river*, from Fly on the Wall Press and *Off the wall*, from Indigo Dreams. She is the author of *Fountain of Creativity: Ways to nourish your writing*, from Victorina Press. She teaches and mentors the writing of poetry and stories: www.writingyourvoice.org.uk

Jenny Robb has poems online and in print including in *The Morning Star; Writing at the Beach Hut; Nightingale and Sparrow; As Above so Below*; in the anthologies, *An Insubstantial Universe* (Yaffle Press) and *Bloody Amazing* (Yaffle and Beautiful Dragons Press) and in the forthcoming anthology, *Lockdown* (Poetry Space).

Caroline Rooney grew up in Harare and now lives in London. She is a writer, filmmaker and activist, and she conducts research on liberation struggles and revolutions. Her poems have been published in several anthologies, mostly recently in *Nicosia Beyond Barriers* (Saqi Books, 2019), and her latest book is *Creative Radicalism in the Middle East: Culture and the Arab Left After the Uprisings* (I.B. Tauris, 2020).

Eddie Saint-Jean is an arts and culture writer and magazine editor by profession and also an award-winning creative writer. His plays and films have had the most recognition in this respect but his recent focus has been poetry, which has provided an equally enjoyable outlet for his creative expression.

Chrys Salt's work has been translated into several languages and has been performed and published internationally. She is Artistic Director of The Bakehouse Community Arts (www.thebakehouse.info) a flourishing arts venue and BIG LIT: The Stewartry Book Festival (www.biglit.org) an annual four day literature Festival in SW Scotland. Chrys was awarded an MBE for Services to the Arts in the Queen's Birthday Honours List 2014.

Barbara Saunders is an English teacher. A poem for refugees appears online (Exiled Ink, 2019) and in a fundraiser, *Over Land, Over Sea* (Five Leaves, 2016). Ekphrastik poems appear in *Mischief and Magic* (Ben Uri Art Gallery, 2018) and Writing on Glass (HLF Sutton Archives, 2018). Her grandparents were Russian Jews.

Joel Scarfe's poems have featured internationally in magazines and periodicals in print and online. He lives in Bristol with the Danish ceramicist Rebecca Edelmann and their two children.

Lily Silverman lived in Hackney between 1980 and 2010. She did her teacher training in Rashan Charles' class, in his primary school, where her son also attended.

Suzan Spence likes exploring many aspects of writing, however, she particularly enjoys attending performance poetry events. Suzan values the use of writing as a means of social comment and has written scripts for the stage. Coming from the Caribbean Diaspora, Black Lives Matter is very close to her heart.

Gerda Stevenson, award-winning writer/actor/director/singer-songwriter, works in theatre, TV, film, radio and opera throughout Britain and abroad: poetry collections include: *If This Were Real* (Smokestack Books, 2013), *Quines: Poems in tribute to women of Scotland*, (Luath Press, 2018); *Inside & Out* (Scotland Street Press, 2019); *Edinburgh* (Allan Wright Photographic, 2019). www.gerdastevenson.co.uk

Laila Sumpton is a half British, half Indian poet, editor and educator working on poetry projects with universities, hospitals, schools, museums and galleries. She is co-leading a new Arts Council funded project called 'Poetry Versus Colonialism' which brings together academics, museum staff, artists, schools and poets to explore colonial history through poetry. She performs at venues across the country and has done commissions for the Tate Modern, Keats House, British Library and Historic Royal Palaces. Laila will soon be publishing a book of poetry with the Arachne Press and is investigating her grandmother's story of Partition through a verse novel.

Samir Sweida-Metwally is a quantitative social scientist at the University of Bristol. His doctoral research - which focuses on the experience of Muslims - examines racism, discrimination and ethnoreligious penalties in the British labour market.

George Symonds works with refugees in the proudly hostile UK immigration and legal aid system, a system that is systemically racist, classist and imperialist. He blogs at www.guiltynation.wordpress.com

Deborah Tyler-Bennett is a European poet and fiction writer, whose forthcoming book of poems is *Ken Dodd Takes a Holiday* (King's England Press, 2021). The volume includes a short sequence on Ella Fitzgerald. She regularly performs her work live and is currently getting used to performing it on online platforms. She's currently finishing her first novel, *Livin' in a Great Big Way*, a story of family secrets, set in the 1940s and '50s. A selection of her poetry is also being translated into Romanian.

Cheryl Vallely is a 57 year old writer who lives in a small market town in Lincolnshire. She is married with a 22 year old son. Poetry has been a passion of hers for many years and she began writing in her early 20s.

In the 1980s **PR Walker** had several poems published in magazines and won a poetry competition. After a gap of over 30 years, he started writing poetry again two and a half years ago. Four recent poems have been highly commended or long-listed in international competitions over the past eighteen months and two have recently been published in The New European.

Patricia Welles is a published writer of six novels and a novelization of a film (Columbia Pictures). She writes plays; one produced at Hampstead Theatre years ago, a public reading at The Theatre Museum, Covent Garden which vanished into the interstices of time. She loves writing poetry and of course reading poetry. There is a rich plethora of poetry by younger black/brown poets across the world. This is a revolution that stimulates other writers to explore poetry. This is the flower that has grown from the weed of prejudice.

Michele Witthaus lives in the United Kingdom. Her pamphlet, *From a Sheltered Place* was published by Wild Pressed Books in 2020 and her poems can also be found in a variety of anthologies and other publications. She is an active member of Leicester Writers' Club.

Kathy Zwick has taught History and Social Studies at international schools in Belgium, Iran, and the UK for over 25 years. The teaching of the "history of history" and new emphasis on all the many perspectives are now more important than ever. Many of her poems recycle themes from old lesson plans.

Acknowledgments

"Species of Reply/Einstein Wasn't Wrong" by Peter A was previously published online in *I am not a silent poet*

"Sunday Read, Cill Rialaig" by Mike Gallagher was previously published in Southword

"Dare to Cross" by Prabhu S. Guptara was published earlier at https://dissidentvoice.org

"Milton-on-the-Hill" by Charles G Lauder, Jr was previously published in *The Aesthetics of Breath* (V.Press, 2019)

A version of the poem, "Any Bus Stop In England" by Paul Lyalls was published in 2003 in 'Velocity' The best of Apples and Snakes (No longer in print)

"No More Silence" by Maureen Mguni was adapted on 11/06/20 from Mguni, M (2020) "Black Lives Matter: No More Silence" https://blogs.brighton.ac.uk/secp/2020/06/09/black-lives-matter-no-more-silence/

The poems "Incident" and "Black Men Should Wear Colour" by Jenny Mitchell were published in her collection, *Her Lost Language* (Indigo Dreams Publishing, 2019)

"Breathe" by Cheryl Moskowitz was previously published in *The New European* 25/6/20

"What the children drew" is included in Hubert Moore's next collection, *Owl Songs* (Shoestring Press, 2021)

"Three Hours" has been published previously in Hubert Moore's latest collection, *The feeding station* (Shoestring Press)

"God I Love My Son" by Loraine Masiya Mponela was first published by Maokwo Arts as part of #RefugeeWeek2020 www.wearemaokwo.com/laura-nyahuye

"Rage rises" by Revd Dr Catherine Okoronkwo appeared on the Bristol Diocese website www.bristol.anglican.org/news/a-personal-response-to-blacklivesmatter.php

"Delivered Into the Arms of the New Normal" by Tracey Pearson was first published in the UK by Hybrid Press 2020, in the 'Race' Dreich Themed Chapbook www.hybriddreich.co.uk

"for George" by steve pottinger has previously appeared on the Culture Matters website under the title "darkening"

"What I Want" by Judith Prest was published online by Writers Resist

"Cotton Thread" by Marilyn Ricci was published in Envoi magazine, 167, June 2012 and Second Light anthology, Fanfare, 2015

"Suffrage" by Jenny Robb was first published in *The Morning Star*, 14/02/2016

"Statue of a South African Woman and Child" was published originally in Gerda Stevenson's book EDINBURGH (Allan Wright Photographic, 2019), a collaboration with Scottish landscape photographer, Allan Wright.

Financial Support

50 people pledged financial support for this project, mainly through our crowdfunder, and enabled us to meet some of the costs associated with bringing the book out. The support is much appreciated.

Printed in Great Britain
by Amazon